EXPLORATIONS

By
Wilma Dykeman

WAKESTONE BOOKS

Some of this material was first
published in the *News-Sentinel* of
Knoxville, Tennessee, and in
The New York Times.

Library of Congress Catalog Card Number: 84-52024
ISBN 0-9613859 - 0 - 1
Published by: Wakestone Books
                405 Clifton Heights,
                Newport, Tennessee 37821

Printed in the United States of America

Books by Wilma Dykeman

THE FRENCH BROAD. A Rivers of America volume.
Holt, Rinehart & Winston.

NEITHER BLACK NOR WHITE. With James Stokely.
Holt, Rinehart & Winston.

SEEDS OF SOUTHERN CHANGE. With James Stokely.
University of Chicago Press.

THE TALL WOMAN. A novel.
Holt, Rinehart & Winston.

THE FAR FAMILY. A novel.
Holt, Rinehart & Winston.

RETURN THE INNOCENT EARTH. A novel.
Holt, Rinehart & Winston.

LOOK TO THIS DAY. Collected Essays.
Holt, Rinehart & Winston.

PROPHET OF PLENTY. *University of Tennessee Press.*

THE BORDER STATES. A Library of America volume. With James Stokely.
Time-Life

TOO MANY PEOPLE, TOO LITTLE LOVE. *Holt, Rinehart & Winston.*

TENNESSEE: A BICENTENNIAL HISTORY. *W.W. Norton.*

HIGHLAND HOMELAND: THE PEOPLE OF THE GREAT SMOKIES.
With Jim Stokely. *National Park Service volume.*

THE APPALACHIAN MOUNTAINS. With Dykeman Stokely.
Text for Graphic Arts photographic study.

TENNESSEE. *Text for a Graphic Arts photographic study.*

WITH FIRE AND SWORD: THE BATTLE OF KINGS MOUNTAIN.
National Park Service.

EXPLORATIONS. A Wilma Dykeman Reader. *Wakestone Books.*

"We shall not cease from exploration
And the end of all our exploring
Will be to arrive where we started
And know the place for the first time."

— T.S. Eliot

Here I stand facing the mountains. The room around me is filled with memories. Memories are bonds with the past. Like all bonds they hold fast and sometimes hurt, but these are also a joining to others: to family, friends, strangers who have no names or faces for me but whose spirits have shared the gamut of experience. Without memories life would be a weaving with no designs, no color, no depth of perspective.

The adjoining room - or two rooms opened into one - is filled with books. Book floor to ceiling, above the doorways, under the desk adapted from a massive old library table, framing the fireplace. Yes, there is a fireplace for adding warmth of several kinds in winter. The books are other worlds, instant transport outside the prison of my own flesh and time. I cannot imagine the starvation of surviving without books.

On the wall behind me is a map. Dark lines draw boundaries around oceans, continents, countries, all the major and minor divisions by which we separate this green whirling planet to fit our human imagination. Blues, greens, pastel colors shade one into another representing Homer's wine-dark seas, Hilary's mountains, Huckleberry Finn's rivers, and land as varied as Hudson's Green Mansions and Lawrence's sun-scorched deserts. Vastness and variety - scenes, smells, sounds, heat and cold - reduced to a dry, stiff bit of cardboard. And wandering like a snail's spoor across an infinitesimal portion of this immensity is a thread of ink: my own tiny trails reaching from this room out, circling back again.

There is a tug-of-war between the hearth and the map, the books and the woods. Two kinds of exploration.

It has all been an exploration: the journeys out, the reaching in, the shining of the many varieties of love - passionately compelling and unpredictable, tenderly enduring with a cobweb's astonishing strength - and the bitterness of disappointment; the unexpected daily wonders and those confrontations which are unique to no one and yet become unique each time they recur - the joy of birth, the grief at death, the everlasting Why?

Is it the Why which makes us human? The Why and the gift of laughter.

Other creatures feed, mate, sleep, seek shelter, communicate and care, form lifetime bonds, rage and grieve. But do the great splendid elephants and apes and cats, the striving bees and ants, the shrewd crows and flashing hummingbirds wonder Why? Or laugh at their own predicament, the audacity and redemption of their questioning?

2

Explorations.

Beginning with this room, with this place on earth, this day and night.

To explore, reaching out from the many roles by which I am defined but never really known, rejecting those definitions which shove complex relationships into narrow pigeonholes.

To explore, identified with but not confined by, this place which is burdened by stereotypes like an ancient ship crusted with generations' accumulation of barnacles.

To explore and share variety, folly, sources of wisdom, comfort, strength.

To ask Why, and to laugh.

Here I stand facing the mountains.

Shaconage — Place of Blue Smoke — the Cherokees called it, the long range of forested pinnacles and plunging valleys crowning the boundary between North Carolina and Tennessee. Eden was the description bestowed by early botanists on this virgin wilderness. But thickets of intertwined laurel and tough rhododendron were known to hunters and settlers as hells.

Today they are the Great Smoky Mountains, encompassed in our country's most popular national park. Like very old friends they possess treasures and offer knowledge overlooked by many who come to call. In contrast are those visitors for whom familiarity breeds content, who return again and again to discover the rich and exquisite diversity of life, the refreshment of wilderness.

3

Recollection of my own first visit to the Smokies is as wrapped in haze as Clingmans Dome on a rainy autumn morning. I was 7 years old and the occasion for the journey was an October fair at the Cherokee Indian Reservation adjoining the Smokies. Southern Appalachia's deciduous hardwood forests were in brilliant color. (How much more poetic was the Cherokees' designation of these scarlet maples, burgundy-red oaks and golden beeches, poplars and hickories as "the trees that lose their hair in winter.")

My parents collected our sturdy old tent that gave off under a noonday sun the pungent smell of ripe canvas and hot tar and cleanliness; gathered up a colorful Double Wedding Ring pieced quilt and a scratchy wool blanket, the skillet, tea kettle and coffee pot bearing scars from past campfires and a book — Horace Kephart's classic study of the Great Smokies *Our Southern Highlanders* — and set forth to make at least nodding acquaintance with an ancient culture and even more ancient wilderness.

Unimportant details of that childhood trip to the Smokies linger in memory today: the muted earth colors of the woven river-cane basket my mother purchased from a Cherokee woman, luxuriant beds of glossy galax and ferns, the looming presence of wild, wooded mountains above the cozy valley where we camped.

Also remaining is an attitude. Attentiveness to small wonders as well as grand spectacles. Appreciation for the unfamiliar, the piquantly different. Respect for the concentrated power that nature may unleash subtly or with unexpected ferocity.

Attitude is important in making acquaintance of the Smokies. They do not present the barren timberline heights or the perpetually snow-capped summits of some other mountain ranges. Their green cover lends them an amiable aura of easy accessibility. But the riches of the Great Smokies

4

have been a long time a-gathering, and they do not yield instantly to the impatient visitor. In the Smokies ordinary things — water, mosses, warblers, rocks — are rendered extraordinary by their abundance, variety, age. Here the commonplace may be transformed into the beautifully uncommon through nature's magic or human ingenuity.

Once inside the park, my discovery of the Smokies usually begins small, with the sound of water. Moving water is the voice of the Smokies. There is no still water here. Not a lake or a pond.

Listen! A melting icicle's metronome drip breaks winter silence along the black slate brows of Alum Cave Bluffs on one of the park's most popular trails.

Listen! Cosby Creek in the park's rugged northeastern corner has "put on its big britches," as mountain folks say, and is roaring down past Cosby campground after a summer storm.

It is an ancient affair, this relationship between water and mountains. We are overhearing only the most recent moment's tick in 200 million years of erosion chiseling the contours of this landscape. The Great Smokies stand as patriarchs among American mountains, already millions of years old when the Rockies and the Sierras and the Cascades were born. And while the altitudes of the Smoky pinnacles are not as breathtaking as those of Western mountains (16 peaks reach above 6,000 feet), their height is imposing because it rises from deep valleys carved by eons of icicles dripping and ages of storm scouring creek beds.

The voice of the water commences as a splattering of raindrops on the polished, leathery leaves of rhododendron and on the dark evergreen of red spruce wilderness, soaking into the deep sponge of centuries-old earth mulch. It bubbles forth from crystal-cold springs whose abundant presence in these hills often determined the site of a pioneer's cabin

5

The rivulets gather into tumbling streams, cascade down boulder-strewn courses to become murmuring rivers as they sweep out of the park, the Oconaluftee across North Carolina's Cherokee reservation, the Little River through Tennessee towns and tourist developments edging the park.

To celebrate the bountiful water of the Great Smokies is to acknowledge its nourishment of the park's distinctive feature: an infinite variety of life. Like the ageless Cleopatra to whom Shakespeare paid that simple and now hackneyed tribute, the Great Smokies charm and entice even as they harbor danger. Their beauty invites further exploration – and demands an accompanying vigilance.

Example: At sunrise atop Mount LeConte, third highest peak in all the Appalachian chain from Canada to Alabama, diaphanous mist wraps the surrounding forest and gentles the outlines of distant ranges. Sunrise spreads a rosy glow over the vast domain. But nearby, along knife-edge ridges slanting down the south slope of LeConte, stretches the wild terrain of Huggins Hell. Known locally as "Laurel slicks," these well-nigh impenetrable tangles can cost the life of the unwary.

Example: Along many of the 800 miles of maintained trail within the park the springtime glory of a bed of delicate pink lady-slipper or a stand of flame azaleas or a summer Turk's-cap lily may surprise the delighted hiker. And around the next curve a timber rattlesnake or a copperhead may be coiled near a rotting log or a rocky ledge. The only two species of poisonous snakes inhabiting the park, their presence requires forethought for each footstep. Blossom and viper are each part of the Smokies' life.

So, too, is the black bear, most popular of the park's creatures – except perhaps with the novice camper who may have been robbed of bacon and chocolate bars.

The bears are large and fascinating. Some weigh 500

pounds and more. Scavenging among trash cans or ambling toward a patch of ripe blackberries in the back country, they appear awkward and clumsy. Not so. The bear is fast and agile. Several have been clocked at racehorse speeds.

Black bears patronize the Newfound Gap thoroughfare across the Smokies, panhandling treats from amateur photographers who brake their cars to a halt and abandon them in mid-highway, creating traffic bedlam known to weary park rangers as "bear jams." The furry, cuddly-looking bear rears up on hind legs and reaches for the goody it expects. This may be photogenic but it is certainly high-risk. Black bears are wild animals, dangerous and menacing if disappointed or threatened. Enjoying the largesse of a law-breaking tourist, the bear wishes to be the one to determine when its snack is finished — and may offer as reminder a slap with his sharp claws. Bears are seldom seen during winter hibernation from December to March, from which the females may emerge every other year with two playful cubs. For them and for all wildlife in the park people must remember that this place is their home. It is the humans who are guests.

Factors other than generous rainfall encourage the diversity of life in the Smokies. Cool northern altitudes in warm southern latitudes make it possible to enjoy the liquid sweetness of a Southern wood thrush's song among lowland beech and birch and maple forests, and a sharp climb and short while later, listen to the raucous cry of the Northern raven in its high wind-battered haunts.

There are 200 species of birds in the park and each year many of them remain throughout the change of seasons. Instead of flying south in the winter those inhabiting the high slopes simply descend to the temperate zone of protected coves. With spring's arrival they return up to the invigorating altitudes of a northern habitat.

Another decisive influence creating a variety of life here

was the ice of a million years ago. The results of this remote event remain a part of the daily landscape of eastern America, influencing construction of interstate highways, location of ski resorts and dams and presence or absence of valuable forest resources.

During the age of glaciers sheets of ice spread down across North America, stopping just short of the southern Appalachians. Plants and animals pushed ahead of the relentless arctic thrust and found refuge in the Great Smokies. Later, as the tongues of ice receded, this southern treasury became the seedbed for desolate northern areas scoured by the glaciers.

Flowering plants, shrubs and trees slowly migrated north again. But they also remained and multiplied in their adopted homeland. There are about 200 species of trees in the Great Smokies today, more than in all of northern Europe. Mast (acorns and nuts) provided by some of the hardwoods support many of the 50 kinds of mammals that roam the park — from saucy squirrels to truculent wild boars.

Thriving, too, in the wake of the ice that herded many of them southward, are 1,500 species of flowering plants. They range from the modest trailing arbutus blooming in hidden crannies to the Catawba rhododendron spreading an imperial purple mantle along favored slopes, and on several of the mysterious grassy balds where forest cover is interrupted for no reason botanists can explain.

Fifty kinds of ferns carpet the Smokies with an elegance and delicacy unmatched by any lace maker. Here 2,000 kinds of mushrooms flourish and 22 salamanders, more species than in any other part of the world. In the park's more than 300 streams are 70 species of fish, including the wily, protected brook trout.

With such a variety of nature's bounty it is little wonder that pioneer settlers accepted isolation and hardship to secure homesteads in these mountains. Thus opens another facet of the Great Smoky Mountains National Park's diversity: its preservation of a human heritage.

In its beginning this was a park with a difference. Before its establishment all 18 of the national parks then in existence were in the Western states, and all had been carved from lands held by the Federal government. But the land to be included in this park had to be purchased from private owners and included more than 6,600 tracts. Many of those owners fiercely resisted parting with their land. Giant paper and lumber companies wished to own the virgin red spruce and other woods that were their raw materials. Small farmers cherished their sturdy cabins, corn patches and apple orchards, pure water and independent ways. But the idea of a national park captured the public imagination.

At that time the Federal Government would not purchase land for national parks. Contributions came from sources characteristically diverse: the pennies and dimes of schoolchildren, appropriations by the states of Tennessee and North Carolina and finally a crucial $5 million gift from the John D. Rockefeller family. Thus, the Great Smokies were not a gift of the government to the people of the United States. In this instance people gave to future generations this park that now embraces 517,000 acres.

Reminders of the people who once called some of these hills and valleys home are still to be found, preserved and displayed as living farms and homesteads.

At the Oconaluftee Visitor Center near the main North Carolina entrance to the park is a pioneer farmstead whose array of barn, smokehouse, cellar, corncrib, pigpen and chicken roost tells the graphic story of mountain self-sufficiency.

On the Tennessee side of the park is Cades Cover, one of the jewels of the Smokies. In this spacious meadowland encircled by an 11-mile loop road 132 families lived a century ago. Here one may enter their way of life, in cabin and farmbouse, small white church and weathered cemetery, creaking gristmill and busy bee gums, grazing cattle and occasional glimpses of wild turkeys or deer or a prowling bobcat. From its grassy fields and bold Abrams Creek, several trails lead to spectacular sites deep in the Smokies.

As with all else in the Smokies, choice of a destination is highly personal. There are summits where views open onto the silence and immensity of successive ranges luxuriantly green in spring and summer, richly tinted in autumn, and in winter, elegantly etched in black and white and dark evergreen. And there are hidden valleys folded in the hills where the voices of the mountains speak to those who listen in splashing streams, wild bird song, whisper of snow.

But seen large or small, these ancient mountains remain ever new. As one old woman who lives within the shadow of the Smokies said recently, "I reckon there's no end to discovering these mountains. I've worn out shoe leather aplenty trying to know them. It keeps me young just wondering what they'll show me next."

Surrounded by a great tumble of jagged grey stones wrenched through the centuries from the encircling mountains, the grey stone hut was almost invisible. Like a reptile patterned to the foliage of its habitat, or the offspring of a majestic beast finding protection in camouflage, this human dwelling glimpsed from a road deep in the mountains of Greece seemed itself to have become part of the wild landscape.

Memory of the temples and shrines, the islands and taverns, the sea and sky of Greece is an invisible treasure which I carry with me and bring forth from time to time and polish and savor. But memory of that stone house is at a deeper level. It forges a kinship.

The kinship is of mountain people. The dweller in this rugged shelter may be a herdsman, probably so, with sheep or goats and the silent rocks and arching sky his companions. More than sixty percent of Greece is mountainous. And along this winding road the loneliness and harshness which lie at the core of life is starkly revealed. In our inventive society of things, devices, objects, such knowledge is hard-won, or never won at all except through vague and disquieting second-hand hints which scarcely penetrate the daily noise and tight routine.

If I ask how the dweller in that crude shelter confronts the grip of winter, the imprisonment of storms, the seeming barrenness of his landscape, I hear echoes of acquaintances who ask how people live in the hills and valleys of the Appalachian ranges - "so far from everything."

What is "everything?" Is it, in fact, every Thing?

If so, then mountains - in Greece, in Appalachia - can bear messages for survival. I remember a son and his wife telling me of meeting a Sherpa woman carrying her heavy burden along steep trails in Nepal, over the rocks, in high thin air, and singing.

Mountaineers in numerous civilizations have been called isolated. Isolated from what? From whom?

11

If you believe that a problem I can best define as one of "regional communication" does not exist in this country, I only wish you might have accompanied me on several recent excursions. Personal and professional commitments have taken me along the East Coast from Florida to New England, not an extremely long distance geographically but in some areas of understanding a wide range indeed - and if the scope is widened to include the Southern Appalachian Mountains, a veritable chasm opens.

In fact, the crevasse becomes apparent in initial social encounters between mountains and ocean. A couple bearing one of the oldest South Carolina names, at home in one of the colonial mansions along Charleston's revered Battery, invites a visitor from the mountains to tea.

"We've always liked that country," the impeccable host says, perhaps addressing his fellow Charleston guests more than his Appalachian visitor. "I have liked it more than my wife does, probably because we used to visit there at a hunting lodge."

"And he always brought back the most marvelous stories of those people . . ." his wife added, her sentence dangling in mid-air.

"Are they changing? Tell us all about those mountain folks."

The visitor might feel like Margaret Mead recently arrived from New Guinea, or one of the old *Harper's Weekly* journalists on horseback penetrating Picturesque America for saleable copy.

Any time a person begins to speak about "those people" - whether the groups are male/female, black/white, Asian/European, affluent/poor, radical/reactionary, etc.etc. - a process of distancing has begun. Gaps are appearing. Concerns are no longer I - you, or we - you, but we/them.

Another gulf appears in New York when a sophisticated

12

and influential new acquaintance says at the beginning of a delectable lunch: "Now tell me exactly where you live. Frankly, I don't know much about the South."

Is it to be magnolias and Scarlett O'Hara's Tara or moonshine whiskey and Tobacco Road? There are so many opportunities for mischief in the presence of such provincialism.

A real abyss yawns during one especially fascinating exchange. The hostess is a European scholar whose knowledge of languages and world geography ranges from Australia's Outback to London's Mayfair, from the Nile in Egypt to New York's Hudson River. She has lived in the United States for the last thirty-five of her many rich years. She is nothing if not candid.

"I have never cared for Southern women," she says, offering a fine paté to her Southern woman guest. "A few years ago I met one on a trip who was delightful. We became quite good friends. But for the most part I don't like those women. And, I must tell you, I am not sure just where the Appalachian Mountains are."

When told that the Appalachian range extends from the Gaspé Peninsula in Canada to northern Alabama she is astonished and suspicious.

"But I have been informed that they are Kentucky and Tennessee and those states. Well, well. So you say that is Southern Appalachia. Well, I shall have to look it up on my maps, find out about that place and those people."

And we return to talking about Izmir and the Gobi and the Galapagos islands.

Yes, there are gaps in our regional communication in this country. Perhaps I should say gaps in regional respect.

Lest I begin to sound paranoid or provincial, however, let me add that encounters with this regional hauteur are not insignificant, especially to those who are being scorned.

13

Raymond Gastil has looked at *Cultural Regions of the United States* and suggested, "The greatest self-confidence and loyalty are inspired in those who see what they do locally in universal terms." Of course.

Such a viewpoint is difficult to achieve if you have been brought to believe, either explicitly or by the power of suggestion, that the place where you live is inferior, out of the mainstream. How to be neither defensive nor offensive about the region where we live?

Gastil spoke to this dilemma. "As long as artists or businessmen or professors in the regional centers of the country see success as achievable only outside their region, there will be no great regional cultures. On the other hand, as long as those who remain in the 'boondocks' see their task as the glorification of whatever characteristics their regions happen to possess, they will build little that is enduring. The Iranian poet Hafez was asked many times to leave Shiraz for India, where the big money was in the fifteenth-century Islamic world; but he stayed behind, where his life was. He has come down to us as a model creator of sheer beauty in poetry, while the poets who went to India are forgotten. Perhaps the greatest creativity comes from remaining at a creative distance from both great population centers and local surroundings and building a universe of one's own."

Wherever your universe may be it will be unworthy if it is ignorant or indifferent or contemptuous of other places.

Recently overheard, a recipe for a happy life: Die young as late as possible.

That summarizes my attitude toward longevity as well as

any phrase I know. And I have known people who died old at forty and young at eighty. If living means more than mere survival, if twenty-four hours add up to something more than another turning of the calendar's page, then I suppose we must seek a balance between the genes we receive and the attitudes we cultivate, between mind and muscles, high spirits and low blood pressure.

Die young as late as possible!

It is difficult to remember that the land we "own" has been bought at many prices, not all recorded in registered deeds.

"Murder is murder, whether committed by the villain skulking in the dark or by uniformed men stepping to the strains of martial musick. Murder is murder, and somebody must answer. Somebody must explain the streams of blood that flowed in the Indian Country in the summer of 1838. Somebody must explain the four thousand silent graves that mark the trail of the Cherokee to their exile."

This angry plea for knowledge of a disgraceful event in America's past, this anguished cry for an awakened conscience, is contained in a remarkable memoir that might well be included in many of our history books. Ownership of land (do we ever really "own" earth?) is almost always won in blood and human sacrifice. Our corner of the Appalachians is no exception.

On a winter day in 1890 John G. Burnett felt the need to share some memories with his children. Here are a few of his thoughts:

"This is my birthday December the 11th 1890. I am

15

eighty years old today. I was born in Sullivan County, Tennessee. I grew into manhood fishing in Beaver-Creek and roaming through the forest hunting the deer, the wild boar and the timber wolf . . . On these long hunting trips I met and became acquainted with many of the Cherokee Indians, hunting with them by day and sleeping 'round their camp fires by night . . .

"The removal of the Cherokee Indians from their life long homes in the year 1838 found me a young man in the prime of life and a private soldier in the American army, being acquainted with many of the Indians and able fluently to speak their language I was sent as interpreter into the Smoky Mountain Country in May 1838 and witnessed the execution of the most brutal order in the History of American Warfare. I saw the helpless Cherokees arrested, dragged from their homes and driven at the bayonet point into the stockades, and in the chill of a drizzleing rain on an October morning I saw them loaded like cattle or sheep into six hundred and forty five wagons and started toward the West.

"One can never forget the sadness and solemnity of that morning. Chief John Ross led in prayer, and when the bugle sounded and the wagons started rolling, many of the children rose to their feet and waved their little hands good-bye to their mountain homes knowing they were leaving them forever. Many of these helpless people did not have blankets, and many of them had been driven from home barefooted. On the morning of November the 17th we encountered a terrifick sleet and snow storm with freezing temperature, and from that day untill we reached the end of the fateful journey on March the 26th 1839, the sufferings of the Cherokees were awful. The trail of the exiles was a trail of death. They had to sleep in the wagons and on the ground without fire, and I have known as many as twenty-two of them to die in one night of pneumonia due to ill treatment,

16

cold and exposure . . .

"The only trouble that I had with anybody on the entire journey to the West was with a brutal teamster by the name of Ben McDonal who was useing his whip on an old feeble Cherokee to hasten him into the wagon. The sight of that old and nearly blind creature quivering under the lashes of a bull whip was too much for me . . . The little hatchet that I had carried in my hunting days was in my belt and McDonal was carried unconscious from the scene . . .

"In May 1838 an army of four thousand regulars and three thousand volunteer soldiers under Command of General Winfield Scott marched into the Indian Country and wrote the blackest chapter on the pages of American History. Men working in the fields were arrested and driven to the stockades. Women were dragged from their homes by soldiers whose language they could not understand . . . "When Scott invaded the Indian Country, some of the Cherokees fled to caves and dens in the mountains and were never captured, and they are there today . . .

"I wish I could forget it all, but the picture of those six hundred and forty five wagons lumbering over the frozen ground with their cargo of suffering humanity still lingers in my memory. Let the Historian of a future day tell the sad story with its sighs, its tears, and dieing groans - let the Great Judge of all the Earth weigh our actions and reward us ac cording to our works.

"Children, thus ends my promised birthday story."

Private Burnett could not forget. Neither must we.

NOW IS the season for Janus, the god who could see in two directions. Looking back. Looking forward.

Tonight we are poised at the equinox between the old and the new . . . between yesterday and tomorrow . . . between the past and future, as bright as a newly minted silver dollar, a fresh snowfall, an unused windshield, a many-faceted diamond.

Does the past hold any meaning that really shapes our daily lives? Does the future conceal any promise that will influence our destiny? Have we any choice whether we shall remember the old and welcome the new?

There are those who say, with the Englishman Oliver Goldsmith, "I love everything that's old — old friends, old times, old manners, old books, old wine."

On the other hand, there are those who would agree with Ralph Waldo Emerson that "Nature abhors the old," and believe the antique proverb, "Newer is truer."

We are told that it is not only the presence of new ideas, habits, modes of living, incredible inventions, that unnerves us now, it is also the rapidity with which these changes arrive. Future shock was diagnosed several years ago but its waves still send tremors through our lives.

As we part with an old year and open another unknown, uncharted bundle of 365 days, there are a few mementoes of the past we might want to keep.

Common Courtesy: Not the empty forms, the mere gestures prescribed by some book of etiquette, but the acts of social kindness and respect that suggest substance, the substance of due regard for one's fellow creatures.

Family Kindness: If one cannot practice acceptance and loyalty to the small family which is known most closely, how can there be true concern for that larger family of humanity involved in our democratic principles and our religious beliefs? The habit of kindness is learned, or forgotten, in that

18

strongest of all classrooms, the home.

Endurance: This does not appeal to quicksilver youth which feels it can vanquish obstacles in one decisive conquest and bring life under its control and desire. But simple stamina, the courage of endurance saluted by William Faulkner in his Nobel Prize speech, is a virtue to be cultivated, to be valued.

And what of the qualities with which we might anticipate the future? Enthusiasm, born not of erratic fads and fading fashions but the abiding high spirit that gives youth of any age a genuine power. Honesty, that freedom from cant and fraud that spurns not only the hypocrisy of others but our own little private hypocrisies.

The ashes of a past year grow cold, the fires of a new year leap into flame. May that new fire warm our hearts and light our ways to experience richer than we have known before.

Opening the door to a new year what gift more choice to share than some polished gems of thought considering the turns of the seasons, the life of earth and water and sky progressing through another twelvemonths?

Let Walt Whitman, who sang so eloquently of America despite his experience in the tragic bloodletting of our Civil War, remind us: "After you have exhausted what there is in business, politics, conviviality, love, and so on — have found that none of these finally satisfy, or permanently wear — what remains? Nature remains: to bring out from their torpid recesses the affinities of a man or woman with the open air - the sun by day and the stars of heaven by night."

May this year bring you renewed communication with

the sun by day and the stars of heaven by night.

Be refreshed by observations of Izaak Walton who long ago wrote the classic *The Compleat Angler,* and told us: "Water is the eldest daughter of the Creation, the element upon which the Spirit of God did first move, the element which God commanded to bring for the living creatures abundantly; and without which those that inhabit the land, even all creatures that have breath in their nostrils, must suddenly return to putrefaction . . . this is the chief ingredient in the Creation . . ."

May you find your thirst quenched by sweet pure waters.

Perhaps his childhood spent here among our Appalachian mountains gave Thomas Wolfe a heightened awareness of the earth and its abundance. He sang of it gloriously, "All things belonging to the earth will never change — the leaf, the blade, the flower, the wind that cries and sleeps and wakes again, the trees whose stiff arms clash and tremble in the dark, and the dust of lovers long since buried in the earth — all things proceeding from the earth to seasons, all things that lapse and change and come again upon the earth — these things will always be the same, for they come up from the earth that never changes, they go back into the earth that lasts forever. Only the earth endures, but it endures forever."

Surround yourself with the harmony and perspective which will let each day be part of the enduring rhythms of the earth.

The English novelist Thomas Hardy wrote of space and the starry deep long before the launching of our moon-bound vehicles. He said, "To persons standing alone on the hill during a clear night such as this, the roll of the world eastward is almost a palpable movement. The sensation may be caused by the panoramic glide of the stars past earthly objects, which is perceptible in a few minutes of stillness, or by the better outlook upon space that the hill affords, or by the wind, or by the solitude; but whatever its origin, the impression of riding along is vivid and abiding."

Find moments of mystery, of solitude, of riding along with a great current of time in invisible but powerful vehicles of awareness, of the spirit.

Finally, may the year bring you the tonic of which Henry Thoreau wrote at Walden Pond: "We need the tonic of wildness, — to wade sometimes in marshes where the bittern and the meadow-hen lurk, and hear the booming of the snipe: to smell the whispering sedge where only some wilder and more solitary fowl builds her nest, and the mink crawls with its belly close to the ground . . . We need to witness our own limits transgressed, and some life pasturing freely where we never wander."

Good seasons to you.

What would you consider one of the riskiest ventures you might undertake today?

Driving on the freeways that have become free-for-alls of survival or destruction?

Opening a business enterprise and entering the rough competition which surrounds any commercial daring?

Playing the roulette wheels in the casinos of Las Vegas or Monte Carlo?

Going to the moon?

One of the chanciest endeavors any of us attempt is marriage.

I seem to have received an unusually large number of wedding invitations and announcements in recent months. (Is June still the most popular month for walking down the aisle or into the J.P.'s office?) But balancing those happy messages are numerous disclosures of separations, letters informing me of broken bonds, shattered promises.

Writers have contemplated the fragility of marriage for many generations. England's Ben Jonson said in 1633: "How like a lottery those weddings are." W.S. Gilbert, of the famous operatta team of Gilbert and Sullivan, observed a couple of centuries later that marriage is "an experiment frequently tried," (Elizabeth Taylor, Mickey Rooney and the Gabor sisters can verify that word "frequently.")

Statistics with which we are all familiar support the conclusion published in a recent report based on thirty years of research: "Odds on any marriage being a success are shorter than those of hitting the jackpot on a pinball machine in Las Vegas."

The report also mentions annulments and desertions and the bleak figures which could be added by "what we call the morbidity marriage where a man and a woman may continue living with each other just for appearances or convenience while actually hating each other."

A useful insight contained in this report suggests that one reason for the high risk rate in marriage is that men and women seek and need different satisfactions. "Companionship is the first subconscious factor influencing the male in mate selection. Then comes sex, love-affection-sentiment in a single category, home and family, and helpmate (one giving encouragement), and, lastly, security."

"For the woman the first things she seeks are love, affection and sentiment. She has to feel loved and wanted. The second is security, then companionship, home and family, community acceptance, and sixth, sex."

Well, well!

If everyone who entered into the "love, honor and cherish" ceremony had some inkling of these facts — that what each partner needs and wants may vary in intensity — a few of the hazards of marriage might be lessened.

Meanwhile, if you feel an urge to gamble go face the hazards of mountain climbing, the horse races, or prospecting for gold. Marriage is too wonderful, too much fun and challenge, too miraculous to place second to a slot machine.

A window in my mother's home overlooks a green hillside and a narrow fern-filled ravine. Tall poplars and smaller sourwood, a giant oak, a sentinel white pine, tower over the clusters of rhododendron and wild azalea and gnarled old laurels.

Arching over the tiny stream which winds between banks of brown leaves and copper-colored galax is a tulip poplar. As long as I can remember it has leaned there — perhaps a few inches lower each year. Its roots still clutch deeply in the earth. Its limbs still put forth a leafy green each spring and summer with rising sap.

And almost as long as I can remember there has arrived, from time to time, the inevitable casual visitor who asks why that tree hasn't been cut.

It is out of place.

It defies standard procedures of both gravity and uprightness.

It grows old.

It threatens to fall.

Because of these facts, and the unique features it brings to the landscape, our slanting poplar is a cherished rebel.

That awry tree symbolizes for me the odd, the unusual, the eccentric which exists in every aspect of nature, revealing itself at unexpected moments for our delight and surprise.

Personally I have never wanted trees that are all straight, streams that uniformly flow in tidy channels, fences that are exactly level, and walkways that are too direct.

A tree with a few bends or twists embodies a history of wrestling with wind, storm, perhaps fire and lightning, the onslaught of man — and a triumph over these encounters. A stream must wander to find its natural bed. Fences should march to the contour of the land, rising or falling with geography. And a walkway may prove that a straight line is the shortest distance between two points — but it isn't necessarily the most interesting.

Thus with the weather, too. The ultimate boredom for me would be to awaken each morning to certain sunshine or perpetual snow. It is the echo of rising wind, the threat of sudden storm, the possibility of balmy warmth, that makes each day fascinating. The only certainty is change. And eccentricity.

Boulders and people who arrest our strongest attention also have some jagged edges. Pebbles and personalities worn too smooth may make satisfactory filler material for garden paths or congregations — but they do not capture our eye or stimulate our minds. It is the grey ledge, rough and precipitous, it is the sharp eye and witty word and work-worn hand which attracts our admiration.

My leaning poplar tree, boldly askew in an upright forest, will someday lose its tenacious grip on the hillside. Meanwhile, a strong new offshoot has already grown from its side — a straight, soaring, smooth limb reaching up to the sun. I'm glad no one tidied the woods and cut away our arching tulip poplar before it produced this offspring.

And when it goes — that odd, gnarled old tree — the hillside and ravine and woods will not be the same. Only the ravages of time and the fortitude of deep roots can pro-

24

duce such an audacious monument to the tenacity and mystery of life.

Consider:

The glazed and sightless stare on many a youthful face; the vacant and inattentive gaze that captures many an elderly countenance; the look of troubled emptiness that seems to afflict many human faces when we glimpse them in unsuspecting moments of repose or reflection.

And consider how many of these outward expressions are mirrors of the inner sickness of boredom.

Boredom is one condition I do not understand. I have endured the normal number of plagues and indulged the usual number of faults experienced by most people, but the misfortune of boredom has not been among my woes. There have always been too many things to do — some pleasant, some unpleasant but necessary — and there has always been too much to learn and know, for me to find any hour or day tedious and unrewarding. And yet, there are numerous indications that boredom may be one of the illnesses which is growing more widespread and aggravated throughout our society.

A century ago one observer warned. "Ennui has made more gamblers than avarice, more drunkards than thirst, and perhaps as many suicides as despair."

25

Can it be that some of the violence and desperation which characterizes so much of our life — including our so-called "recreation" — is really the reflection of a sense of loss of purpose which infects our work and play? The Frenchman, Pascal, concluded: "There is nothing so insupportable to man as complete repose, without passion, occupation, amusement, care. Then it is that he feels his nothingness, his isolation, his insufficiency, his dependence, his impotence, his emptiness."

The youth who will not share the memories and wisdom of age, the elderly person who will not try to understand the search and hope of adolescence, the person anywhere who will not awaken to the passionate concerns and the need to care which surrounds him — these are ready victims of boredom, tedium, ennui. And that is a sort of death-in-life. It is isolation, impotence, emptiness.

Boredom is a sort of arthritis of the imagination, a paralysis of the spirit.

IN THE SAME MAIL last week I received printed matter that contained contrasting messages. The first was on a personal card. It said: "Dear Lord — bless the beasts, the singing birds, And every life that has no words." The second was incorporated in an impersonal magazine article. It stated: " . . . the average American youth will witness 11,000 TV

26

murders by the time he is 14." Gentleness and violence. Life versus death.

Can we confront these poles in our lives — as individuals and as a society — and choose with constant consciousness and determined conscience a course that will attest to pride in our humanity, a vision of divinity? In a hundred different ways the grim communiques are imparted: A battered child's broken bones; a friend's clinched fist as he discussed a competitor; revolution in some small distant nation; slaughter of elephants for their tusks and leopards for their skins to decorate a dilettante's flesh; a neglected grandparent's broken spirit; everyday unkindness and hidden raw brutality; the inhumanity of much of our "entertainment:" Movies, sports, books, television, comics — on and on. We are violent and we are nurturing that violence. We feed it to our children as surely as we feed them proteins and vitamins. And if we watch, the results are equally apparent.

But we are also gentle. We can be moved by suffering. We respond to needs of others. Where — in our world of multi-million-dollar prize fights and our contempt for the "do-gooder" and our short-changing of service-oriented professions — where is the glamourizing of the merciful, the generous, the kind, the hopeful and the helpful?

At the threshold of a new year I would like to raise this one small toast to all the gentle folks around the world.

Our reliance in this fresh new year still seems to lie, as it has through so many ages of the past, in the gun and the dollar (or the gold.) We will protect our possessions and we will win friends, next door or around the world, with the power of our money. And if we cannot win influence with cash we can always exercise the strength of mighty arsenals. Tucked away in our minds is final trust in the gun: The one we own ourselves or the big bang of the bomb which belongs to us all. Our faith lies in our capability for violence.

27

Is this the source of ultimate power? Or does it carry, for an individual or a society, an awful potential for self-destruction? Our violence feeds upon itself and gnaws at our vitals.

Yet we continue to neglect and misunderstand the gentle men and women. They are not the weak, not the stupid or the apathetic. They have the greatest of all authority — control over themselves and confidence so unshakeable that it does not need the trivial adulation of a fickle public. They are not the ineffectual citizens of our world; they are simply the ones who do not believe that it is necessary to mix another's blood, sweat or tears into the cement on which they construct their own pedestal. They believe that true supremacy flows from mutual respect, sincere and sustained effort at understanding, generosity of spirit, the courage to be kind to each living creature.

To such as these, then, an especially Happy New Year. May they find honor among us for offering alternatives to our violence-wracked society.

What is it we receive at birth and keep until death - indeed, until after death as it is the only part of us that lives on in the world?

What is it that we forget most often, causing us to lament most loudly our forgetfulness?

What carries with us each day of our lives a freight of history, meaning, beauty or humor, honor or dishonor, memory?

Let us consider names.

We each have two names, one inherited and one given, designating our membership in a family and our individuality as a unique person. Sometimes we have additional names: a middle name, a nickname, a title specifying our profession or distinction of status. Thus we become Sandy or Shorty or Blondie, Stonewall (as in Jackson) or Dizzy (as in Dean). Or we are Judge, Doctor, Professor; Lord and Lady, Sir or Bishop.

Which are the most common surnames in the United States? Smith far outnumbers all others, but the next ten are: Johnson, Brown, Miller, Jones, Williams, Davis, Anderson, Wilson, Taylor, and Thomas. (Perhaps you thought Jones was the second most popular name?)

Choosing given names for our children we are influenced by many considerations. We want to honor someone (a dear grandparent or an old friend), we like the harmonious sound (Oliver Wendell Holmes), we favor some object (Rose, Pearl, Leo as in lion), we want to recall some place or event (Savannah, Liberty, Waterloo), or we celebrate a biblical name or a virtue (Matthew, Mark, Luke and John; Faith, Hope and Charity). Surely the name registered by an Ohio draft board a few years ago incorporated a wide range of given names: Noah Harvey Herman Daniel Boone Buster Brown David Longworth. (Wonder what the boy's nickname was?)

Did you know that there are many more names for girls than for boys? Among the reasons for this is the fact that many boys' names can be adapted for girls by adding "ella," "etta," "ina" and similar feminine endings while very few girls' names can be adapted to masculine forms.

For centuries now the most popular girl's name in the Western world has been Mary. In Arabia it takes the form Maryam, in Greece Mariam, in Hawaii Mele, in Scotland Mor, and in numerous countries from Denmark to Mexico it is Maria. Next in order of longtime popularity have been: Elizabeth, Barbara, Dorothy, Helen, Margaret, Ruth, Virginia, Jean and Frances.

Almost as popular as Mary for the girls is John for boys. Jehan in Belgium, Jean in France, Jussi in Finland, Sean in Ireland, Giovanni in Italy, Ivan in Russia, Evan in Wales, John is joined in high popularity by William. Other most familiar names are Charles, James, George, Robert, Thomas, Henry, Joseph and Edward.

Many humorous stories are attached to names. When a clergyman in England was asked to christen a baby "Sirs," the parent gave as the Scriptual source for this puzzling name the passage from Acts: "Sirs, what must I do to be saved?"

Ecclesiastes says that "A good name is better than precious ointment," suggesting that whatever name we are given it is what we add to its meaning that makes it live in honor or disrepute.

Sigmund Freud, the founder of psychoanalysis, says that we forget certain names for reasons often unknown to us. Considering the lamentations I hear, we are all open to psychoanalysis in this matter.

Your name: is it "rather to be chosen than great riches?"

IN THAT LONG-AGO land where I was reared people still remembered the worn adages which were supposed to help us grow better and better every day in every way. A large number of these proverbs had to do with thrift. "Waste not, want not" was the briefest and bluntest summary of a whole covey of mottoes which adorned our minds — and sometimes our desks and walls as well.

Recently it has occurred to me, however, that the fates guiding my destiny do not seem to be as familiar with this old saw as I am. As I make my own small effort to live up to

George Bernard Shaw's warning, "The love of economy is the root of all virtue," I am ambushed and undermined.

Let me share some failures in my small efforts to save time or miles or money.

Time is our most precious possession. Without it all other resources are useless. Time is life itself. Impressed by this fact — and the relentless gallop of the clock and calendar — I recall the motto, "A stitch in time saves nine." Not with me, it doesn't. As when I try to save a minute in one of the lines forming at the grocery store counter or the bank window.

As I approach the several lanes open for use I try to make a rapid survey of the contents of the wire baskets or the financial documents clutched in each hand of those ahead of me, as well as the length of the line. Having chosen the queue that seems most likely to save me a few minutes I take my place and wait. And wait. And wait. It turns out that the little lady with only a box of prunes and a jar of wheat germ in her grocery cart must write a careful check for the $1.79 bill and then she wants to count the green stamps and tuck them neatly in a zippered compartment of her purse before she leaves.

Or, at the bank it develops that the man who had only one innocent looking bit of paper in his hand suddenly fishes from a coat pocket a leather case and dumps a mound of unassorted money before the teller. From the size of the currency it appears that he must hold the bubblegum concession for several counties. While other lines on either hand move forward with a steady pace I watch pennies being racked up and sheathed in paper holders. My effort to save time is a slow-boiling wretched failure.

Then I decide to save miles. "Cut the suit to fit the cloth," the wise ones warned in earlier days, so why not today cut the journey to fit the roads. I consult a map and notice that there are several short cuts on my next journey.

I might save a dozen or so long miles. By the time I have wound up in several back yards with barking dogs and curious children, by the time I have encountered a lengthy detour (reassuring me with a sign which says, "Today's inconvenience is tomorrow's progress"), I decide that saving mileage is not "the root of all virtue."

As for thrift with money — well, we know that "a penny saved is s penny earned." For me a penny saved is often a penny lost. I find a sale, I discover incredible bargains — and shortly after I stock up on the great money-saving items, I find that they have been declared, by some unseen but potent authority, to be either unstylish, unhealthy or unsafe. My pennies saved are dollars lost!

On the larger scale, I'm sure that the admonition of my childhood, "Waste not, want not," must be true. Think of all we waste in America and how much we're still wanting. But somehow I wish that it might be just a little easier to waste not.

"No weather's ill if. the wind be still."

The Englishman who made that observation more than two centuries ago spoke for me. Sun or rain, thunder or snow, each brings its moments of excess and crisis — but even the mildest breeze is capable of arousing foreboding, at least for me.

And I am not alone in my response to wind. Around the world there are names given to various winds distinctive to mountain and desert places. I have written about this before but my attention was brought to bear again by the fierce winds which have lashed our hill this spring, torn stout limbs from tall white pines, and reminded us that nature's power is still paramount in this world. I have noted, too, a business article which discussed the recent rise in cocoa prices around the world (as reflected in that box of chocolates you bought). Why should cocoa be in short supply? A major factor is the harmattan, a dry wind that blows from the Sahara desert over the cocoa trees in Africa's ivory coast, one of the world's major producers of cocoa. Thus a dust-laden wind on the Atlantic coast of a distant continent affects our cupboards and deserts.

In Africa it is the harmattan.

In France it is called the mistral.

In Switzerland, Austria and Southern Germany it is known as the fohn.

In Israel it is named the sharav.

In Arab countries it is the hamsin.

In Treste it is titled the bora.

Whatever its designation, it is the wind. A special wind, often bearing disaster, but akin to our own spring gales.

Those of us who find strong winds unsettling, even distracting, may be comforted to know that we have sound reasons for our reactions. Israeli doctors have found that the sharav brings very real suffering to many dwellers in that country. Depression, headaches, breathing difficulties, flaring tempers. Experts at the Hebrew University in Jerusalem have estimated that one-half of the adult population of that city "experiences undesirable reactions to the sharav." Research is under way to find medicines and instruments which may help alleviate these conditions.

Perhaps the best known of all these winds is the mistral. A number of years ago our family encountered the mistral during a visit to Avignon in Southern France. The gusty blasts drove shifting patterns of clouds across the sky. The mistral stirred deep swells and waves upon the gray waters of the Rhone River rushing beside the city. It rose and plunged around the medieval walls and towers of the imposing papal palace and through the narrow streets. Although the season was summer, the chill of those winds drove us to find sweaters and coats.

Later, we learned that in courts of law a criminal may draw a lighter sentence if he can prove that the crime of passion occurred when the mistral was blowing.

Let me acknowledge that the winds are a part of nature's master plan; they bring variety to our lives. Without them the world would be less interesting. In this spirit I paraphrase the familiar old Irish prayer: "May the road rise with you, and my the harmattan-mistral-fohn-sharav-hamsin-bora be always at your back!"

A FEW PEOPLE can't read. Others won't read. Too many don't read.

It grieves me to think about the strength and joy I have received from great minds through reading that will never be known to others who do not discover this experience. I am also disturbed by the fact that I do not refresh myself more often at the springs of ancient wisdom. Efforts to keep up with what is current distract me from much that is eternal.

A Midas may draw the blinds over the windows of his counting house, lock the doors, and find some sort of satisfaction in measuring gold and bonds, stocks and money market funds. But there is another kind of treasure which brings pleasure when the windows are thrown open, the doors invite entrance, and sharing is the touchstone.

I would share such riches of the mind that I have found memorable through the years. Brief, wise, sometimes humorous, these are words distilled from experience, common sense, uncommon insight, and skill in communicating truths which apply to all of our lives. Consider happiness:

Abraham Lincoln said, "Most folks are about as happy as they make up their minds to be." And the Greek Plutarch told us, "A pleasant and happy life does not come from external things; man draws from within himself, as from a spring, pleasure and joy."

The English writer J.B. Priestley told us something familiar but no less true today than yesterday: "To me there is in happiness an element of self-forgetfulness. You lose yourself in something outside yourself when you are happy; just as when you are desperately miserable you are intensely conscious of yourself, are a solid little lump of ego weighing a ton."

I can carry those images in my mind for days: a wellspring from which I may draw the living waters of joy — or a solid little lump of ego weighing down my spirit and my feet.

"We cannot walk through life on mountain peaks," naturalist John Burroughs observed. Although it is our moments on the peaks that many friends and family see, the real challenge comes in how we meet the experiences in the lonely valleys. Here we find our courage — or lack of it.

It is the ordinary, daily, garden-variety courage that receives too little attention and cultivation in our lives. Yet Robert Louis Stevenson advised, "Keep your fears to yourself, but share your courage with others." And Greek wisdom told us that "Danger can never be overcome without danger." If fear is contagious, courage too may be catching. Perhaps we need to remember the words of the crusty old philosopher of Walden Pond, Henry David Thoreau: "Men were born to succeed, not to fail." (Women, too.)

In fact, I could sift through Thoreau's nuggets for days. Try a few of these on for size:

"Be not simply good; be good for something."

"A man is rich in proportion to the number of things he can do without. Beware of all enterprises that require new clothes." (Does this apply to women, too?)

"Simplicity, simplicity, simplicity . . . Simplify, simplify . . . "

— and draw on gems of thought from noble minds.

"PATTERNS ARE for cloth and paper dolls," a friend remarked, "Deliver me from people who cut themselves to a pattern."

When I visit my mother's home in Asheville I drive along a stream that I remember from my childhood. It has changed — or to be more accurate I should say that it has been changed. It has been reshaped to a pattern.

From a winding watercourse that once found its way between rhododendron-covered banks, among moss-covered rocks, along a meandering route, it has been transformed into a straight, efficient, uninteresting canal.

Gone are uneven patches of landscape where an unpredictable slope diverted the stream into a different direction. Gone are the clutching roots of tall old trees whose tentacles sought to hold earth fast from the pull of rushing water. Gone are the tiny pools and miniature rapids formed by the altering pace and course of the waterway.

Someone wanted everything regular, even, conforming.

And someone erased all that was distinctive and fragile and beautiful about that brook.

And yet . . . the world's art, the great scientific discoveries have been created when someone broke the pattern, when someone's thoughts meandered, found pools of time in which to reflect, imagine.

Reading the history of treasured Persian rugs, we are told of the individual labor and care lavished on each specimen. "A good carpet takes months, sometimes years, to weave; a few are the work of a lifetime. Irregularities in patterns and colors, strangely enough, often count for the Persian rug's beauty and brilliance. Power looms can weave fairly exact copies, but the product lacks vitality and luminosity."

Vitality and luminosity: the quality of life itself.

With rugs, with streams, with people: How often it is the irregular, the uneven, the unusual and the unexpected that creates interest and lasting value.

Sometimes it has seemed that our world of "feminine beauty," for instance, was intent on manufacturing faces that all look alike — or as closely alike as nature would permit. Edicts on eyebrows and lipstick, hair and clothing, make us look more like one another than like ourselves. Yet it has often been the exception that made a face memorable: The slightly high forehead, the unusually intense color of the eyes, the aquiline nose, the uncommonly slender throat, the overly generous mouth. Though we tend to forget it and try to obliterate differences, with our faces as with the Kerman carpets it is irregularity in pattern that may account for beauty and brilliance.

May not the same hold true for thought and character? Those who never put forth the effort to think for themselves are doomed to the dullness of living always by others' standards and conclusions. Those who are fearful of others' opinions will never try new patterns of discovery in the daily routine of their lives. If a good carpet requires months, sometimes years, to weave, how much longer may we need to weave a character, create a face?

Let us leave a few streams free to wander out of ordered channels. Let us leave a few people free to be unique – and pioneer new frontiers for us. Let us leave areas of our own lives unpatterned – vital and luminous.

THE BULK of my medical knowledge comes from the received wisdom of several well-aged home remedy volumes, experience of dealing with numerous aches and pains afflicting the young and the elderly and the in-between, and the magazine and newspaper articles which keep us abreast of the latest discoveries in medical science. I am sure this hodgepodge of misinformation and what is known as "common sense" makes me the despair of many of my doctor friends, as well it might.

During a recent journey I added to my self-help information. The theme of the article was therapy afforded by expressing anger. Putting a lid on all of our resentments and hostilities can cause later explosions and physical symptoms that may seem unrelated. The solution, of course, is to find non-destructive ways in which to vent our minor irritation or our major wrath.

Admittedly, this is not exactly a fresh idea, but sometimes it is useful to be reminded of familiar facts. Let us then consider healthy anger.

There are many ways by which a person reveals character. Sometimes we even surprise or shame ourselves by the unexpected acts we commit and attitudes we express. Perhaps one of the more interesting aspects of a person's personality is revealed by an answer to the question: On what do I spend my anger?

Someone who is never angry is someone who is only half-alive. On the other hand, a Scottish proverb warns, he that will be angry for anything will be angry for nothing. The welcome balance lies in the choice between perpetual rage and righteous indignation.

Considering the alterations that take place in our blood pressure, heartbeat, muscle tensions, and other bodily functions when we are irritated, it is imperative that we choose the objects and causes for which we will sacrifice certain comforts and normality. Are the objects of our temper little daily annoyances that should be overlooked by anyone who has left the crib and its infantile tantrums? Do we choose instead to spend the energy and time consumed by anger on something worthy of its demands? Does a red light at the wrong moment, a stupid play by a bridge or tennis partner, a thoughtless act by friend or neighbor, send us into a brief fury? Or do we reserve that blood, sweat and steam for protest at cruelty and injustice and human indifference to each other's needs?

If we are known by the company we keep, we are also known by the pettiness or largeness of our angers. All of us know people who are never disturbed in the serenity of their days as long as nothing impinges on their own personal comfort or pocketbook. But let something unpleasant or demanding confront them and they are suddenly whirlwinds of vexation and rage.

Aristotle once said, "We praise a man who is angry on the right grounds, against the right persons, in the right manner, at the right moment, and for the right length of time." If we always applied these standards think of the plunge in temper and temperature that would take place

39

in homes and offices, clubs and courtrooms, churches and classrooms everywhere.

Next time anger threatens to engulf you, remember it can be healthy; it may be important. And ask yourself this question: Will this matter tomorrow? A month from now? Perspective helps in channeling our emotions into wise channels.

The agony of seventh grade arithmetic remains a clear and present horror in my memory.

I see the book as clearly as today's newspaper: A nondescript blue cover, pages of unrelieved questions as neatly laid out as stones on the path to the guillotine, my name written in the front with a jaunty curlicue on the first initial diminishing to a brave and irrelevant little period as afterthought.

And those questions! They were about flagpoles which cast shadows of certain lengths at noontime and trains that ran at stated speeds on level ground. Where would the flagpole's shadow fall at 3:00 in the afternoon and how far would the train go on an uphill pull? All of these descriptions involved fractions and left me with an almost irresistible impulse to say that the sun didn't shine on that flagpole and the train ran only in Iowa corn country.

With only 10 fingers to serve in my computations I slaved away many a golden autumn afternoon and many a greening springtime weekend overwhelmed and repelled by numbers. Their message to me was clear and accepted: Trouble.

At last two rays of light penetrated this darkness. For one shining, glorious moment I found my Camelot in algebra.

All the mystery was as clear to me as a first grade reader.

I whizzed through problems. I was even invited by the teacher (obviously as overwhelmed by this miracle as I was) to explain certain steps and answers to the class. Heady stuff.

And then, years later (obviously a slow learner), I was shown the marriage of music and mathematics. The moment of revelation was splendid and decisive. There were unsuspected relationships that existed in various fields of knowledge. Discovering these relationships could make a difference in life — could, perhaps, turn fear of subject matter into eager curiosity.

To a much lesser degree there was also the problem of history and boredom. Kings and queens, explorers and inventors followed each other in orderly succession; the terror, despair, triumph of their lives hardly suggested in the brackets (date of birth and death) which we memorized. Peace followed wars and wars followed peace while we yawned and waited for recess and an exciting game of hopscotch.

Then one day some of us took our mother's second-best sheets to school, dressed up in percale togas and reenacted the death of Julius Caesar. This was murder! As Caesar died of his stab wounds history came alive. Questions of power and government crossed our minds.

These simple personal experiences are not unrelated to complex educational questions confronting us today. Having heard as a child during the Great Depression many of the arguments concerning the purposes, the necessities and the "frills" of education, I become attentive when I hear the old arguments of the practicality of technical and professional training versus liberal arts education. The choice is not either/or. It is both. People must know how to make a living. They must also know how to make a life.

41

As students making continuing choices among our educational opportunities, as parents and teachers struggling to provide guidance and perspective, as administrators balancing demands with resources, as taxpayers or donors contributing to the educational system, and as citizens in a country seeking the maturity to govern itself wisely and justly — we must not, cannot dilute the strength of our liberal arts commitments.

It is useful to remember a definition of the term: "Liberal arts is a translation of Latin 'artes liberales,' so called not because they were liberal in any modern sense of the word, but because their pursuit was the privilege of the freemen who were called 'liberi.' " And the root of the word also means to liberate in the largest sense.

"Self-knowledge," as one educator recently said, "has always been one of the central concerns of liberal education." But in this "age of belt-tightening" it must be emphasized that "more than the fulfillment of individuals is at stake. The welfare of our society and the resilience of our culture and economy depend upon the existence of people whose intellect, values and perspective transcend the particular requirements of the moment. The contributions such people can make because of their broad-ranging capacity and scope is a national asset of the first order."

Reflecting the vitality and centrality of the liberal arts in a free society is the growing awareness of their relationship to the modes of thought represented by analytic skills and technological skills in our culture, our civilization.

A new dialogue is opening. Stephen White of the Alfred P. Sloan Foundation has pointed out: "What the computer has done is provide scope for analytical skills that has never before existed, and in so doing it has altered the world in which the student will live as well as the manner in which he will think about the world. It is these basic facts that con-

42

stitute the link between the computer and liberal education."

I feel as uneasy with computers as I did with seventh grade math. I am a cripple limping in a race with the fleet of foot. Perhaps that is why I care that others should learn young and learn well in the liberal arts. We neglect such liberation at peril to ourselves and our national well-being.

GHOST STORIES have been one of the favorite pastimes and entertainments of humankind through the ages. Witches and uneasy spirits roaming the realms between daylight and darkness are part of our oral heritage and our great literature.

Shakespeare's witches are an important part of his *Macbeth.* They not only create an atmosphere of dread and foreboding, they arouse in Macbeth himself the dark ambition and lust for power that will prove his downfall. They foretell the signs by which his tragedy will unfold.

And in *Hamlet* it is the ghost of his father, roaming the battlements of his unhappy castle, that spurs the young Prince to investigate the death of his father, the remarriage of his mother.

Whether or not Shakespeare believed that witches and ghosts were real, he knew that the inner evil which can destroy a person is real; the voices of doubt and suspicion that inhabit our minds can drive us into profound questioning, under certain circumstances.

I was brought to thinking about this subject by a conversation I had recently with a 95-year-old man in Kentucky. He told me about a number of things of which I had never heard. Among them was the "ghuroo." (I am not certain of that spelling. Neither was he. The word is pronounced the same as "guru," but he said he spelled it in the above fashion.)

When he was a boy, my friend said, his black neighbors told him about the ghuroo. These were witches, of both sexes, who lived in caves or dugouts or other similar places of damp and dark - some shelter and came out only at night. They grew long fingernails that made their bony hands appear to be claws, and with these they dug out fresh graves and ate the bodies interred there. Sometimes they would have to roam the countryside for many miles before they could find their victims.

The ghuroo always chose mules on which to pursue their sinister errands. This was "proved" by the fact that in summer the mules on the farms were always thinner, more worn down than the horses in the neighborhood. Their condition proved that they had been taken out of the stalls or the barn lots at night and ridden by evil spirits.

(As my elderly friend pointed out, the fact that mules were used for the hard field labor in the summer while many of the horses were used only for riding or to pull carriages made no difference in the "proof" of their relation to the ghuroo needs.)

If this story seems grisly, it is no more so than many that were told around the winter's fire in pioneer cabins and later homes of considerable elegance. As a matter of fact, such tales still fascinate readers and listeners in many parts of the world. The similarity between ghost stories provides a common denominator among many nationalities and races.

ARE YOU FAMILIAR with the work of Charles Dodgson?

Is the writing of Christopher Crowfield well known to you? Or a book by Eric Arthur Blair?

What about the world masterpieces of Jozef Teodor Konrad Nalecz Korzeniowski or of Captain Clutterbuck and Rev. Dr. Dryasdust?

Probably none of these names rings a bell in your memory, but chances are you know their books. The Rev. Dr. Charles Dodgson wrote the children's classics, *Alice in Wonderland* and *Through the Looking Glass.* Christopher Crowfield was the name assumed by *Uncle Tom's Cabin* author, Harriett Beecher Stowe, when she wrote her book on etiquette entitled *House and Home Papers* in 1865.

Eric Blair published his famous story of a totalitarian future, *1984,* under the name George Orwell. And Jozef Teodor etc. etc. was the Polish master Joseph Conrad. Clutterbuck and Dryasdust were both names assumed by Sir Walter Scott at some time in his long career.

Pseudonyms come into use for a wide variety of reasons. Personal traits and unfortunate experiences account for a number of authors wishing to remain unknown. Such was the case with North Carolina resident William Sidney Porter who was once convicted of embezzling $1000 and sent to jail. The stories he wrote in prison became known to generations of readers under the pen name of O. Henry.

So, too, with the witty and elegant English playwright and poet, Oscar Wilde, who was imprisoned on a morals charge, When his moving poem, *The Ballad of Reading Gaol,* (with its famous refrain, "All men kill the thing they love") appeared in 1898 it was signed simply by "C.3.3" Wilde had been in the third cell on the third landing of gallery C while in prison.

Attitudes of society are reflected in the need for writers to use pseudonyms. This has been especially and acutely true in the case of many women writers who found it necessary to use a man's name if they were to get their work published and read and judged with any semblance of fairness.

It is interesting that two of Western literature's best known women novelists chose the first name of George. George Sand was Amantine Lucile Aurore Dupin, whose novels spanned the decades from 1832 to the latter part of the 19th century and were forerunners of the social or "problem" novel. Her love affairs were almost as numerous as her novels — and as famous, especially her devotion to the composer Chopin. Sand's contemporary, George Eliot, was really Mary Ann Evans, an English scholar and intellectual whose studies of social change and problems included the ever familiar *Mill on the Floss* and *Silas Marner.*

The attitude of the 18th and 19th century in frowning upon "female writers" influenced one of the early novelists of Southern Appalachian "local color." Mary Murfree took the name Charles Egbert Craddock when she began selling her stories of mountain life to Boston's *Atlantic Monthly* magazine in the latter part of the 19th century. After the publication of her first book in 1884 she became one of America's most successful authors.

And, of course, the man who is considered by many to be the greatest novelist America has yet produced published *Tom Sawyer* and *Huckleberry Finn* and other works under the name Mark Twain rather than his own, Samuel Clemens.

Perhaps there is an urge in each of us, whether we be writers or not, to enjoy brief (or lengthy) periods of anonymity. The difference between us and the famous figures just mentioned is that their "anonymous" masks became better known than their real names. Would you like that?

The interval since dinner has been brief. The last sips of coffee are being savored. One of the guests glances tentatively at his wife.

"We should be going . . . in a few minutes . . . " they say in unison.

And you prepare yourself for the Lingering Farewell. Not only has your friend's remark suddenly blocked the flow of a free and easy evening and dampened down a lively conversation, it has also alerted you to his condition. This condition can be diagnosed as the long good-bye, or the General MacArthur fadeaway. ("Old soldiers never die, they just fade away," is not intended for brisk leave-taking.)

What are the symptoms of Lingering Fearwell? How does it run its course? What are its aftereffects?

Symptoms are unobtrusive and deceptive unless they are early recognized for what they are. For instance, if someone says upon arrival at your door, "Now we can't stay long . . ." is it polite to inquire, "How long?" But his or her statement paralyzes the visit. On one hand, there can be no relaxation because the time is already limited. On the other hand, there is no authentic urgency. Indecisiveness is the word that best describes these symptoms.

When someone glances at her watch and murmurs, "What time is it anyway?" What is the proper response? If you tell the hour and minute without protests there is the suggestion you are rushing her away. If you tell the time but urge her to disregard it, you are simply asking for a repeat performance after a little while.

Then there is the person who warns, "I ought to be on my way . . ." and then lights up another cigarette or draws the footstool closer to his chair for more comfort. Do you reply to his words or to his actions? They clearly contradict each other.

Heralded by such symptoms how does this affliction run its course? Slowly . . . slowly . . .

There are numerous false alarms and several advances and retreats. Women are particularly adept at the latter. "Oh, I forgot to tell our hostess . . ." (disappearing into another room). "Did I tell you about the last long letter from . . ." (fishing into her purse).

The secret of the true practitioner of the Lingering Farewell is to keep as many people as possible on their feet, preferably before an open door letting in its blasts of chill during winter or its waves of heat in summer.

A skilled artist at Delayed Leavetaking can be sure that he will be remembered. Among the aftereffects are weary legs, benumbed conversation, and − if he manages his maneuvers at the door with professional irresolution − possibility of pneumonia for the host.

Nothing is more delightful than entertaining friends and family − and we do not like to see them leave. But, like surgery, the deed needs to be done decisively, quickly.

Good-bye.

Some years ago I discovered a "psychological study" which interpreted a person's personality according to the color which was his-her favorite. From time to time since then I have had people ask me to interpret their own characters and attitudes according to this formula. For those who like a quick-fix on themselves, then, I share this diagnosis."

Let us admit it. We are a nation of curbstone psychologists and amateur psychiatrists. We are fascinated by the easy handbooks and thumbnail sets of rules which allow us to analyze ourselves - and especially our friends.

We devour books and articles which claim to provide insight into our "innermost selves," the unknown impulses which drive us and the unsuspected influences which control us. We like new formulas by which we can interpret the astonishing actions and characters of those we know and most especially of ourselves.

A new tool for the amateur psychologist has just come to hand. It is as simple as it is intriguing. It ought to provide conversational material for at least one family meal or an exchange over the lunch table.

A large company has published a chart which suggests the general personality of the person who cherishes a certain color. Here is the analysis:

The person who prefers Blue is listed as : Conservative, loyal, reflective, self-controlled and conscientious.

For Orange the personality is: Friendly, extroverted, sympathetic, fickle, and light-hearted.

Red is the preference of those who are: Optimistic, dramatic, imaginative, temperamental and romantic.

Green attracts the personality that is: Well-balanced, a nature lover, conventional, faithful and ambitious.

The person who choose Yellow is: Visionary, aloof, avant garde, intellectual and passive.

The characteristic of those who prefer Violet: Aristocratic, resplendent, artistic, moody and elusive.

Well, there in a nutshell (or a color wheel) is your personality. Do you recognize yourself?

The difficulty arises when you meet a person who insists on two favorite colors, of equal attraction, and they are Orange and Yellow. How do you manage to be friendly, sympathetic, extroverted and fickle while being at the same time aloof, intellectual, avant garde and passive?

This chart described me exactly. I simply looked under my favorite color and accepted all the favorable characteristics and rejected those which were unattractive (and obviously incorrect)! I advise you to follow the same course.

IT IS EASY and often fashionable to become pessimistic over the "state of the world" in which we live. Improvement of the human condition seems more illusory than real; progress is merely a word; cynicism assures us that our efforts to advance are actually retreats before the complex problems engulfing us.

No one would deny that injustice, immorality, suffering, and dilemmas abound. But it impairs our concern, it undermines our commitment if we do not recognize that we do have successes. To deplore only our failures without celebrating some of our achievements is to distort history and destroy the human capacity for hope.

Two recent items in the news provide reason for a sense of accomplishment and affirmation. First, a hunter in Oregon cut his finger on a bone of a rabbit he had just killed and contracted bubonic plague, but state medical authorities announced that he recovered and returned to work. Second, it is now believed that smallpox has been eradicated from this earth.

We tend to find it difficult to value something that does not happen as much as something that does take place. But when we consider the impact that these two dread diseases have had on the human race we can only offer thanksgiving for all the dedication, labor, knowledge that contributed to their abolition from the annals of suffering and waste.

The history of bubonic plague — or the Black Death as it was called during its appalling harvests of death through centuries — serves as grim reminder of the interlocking destiny of all peoples on our planet. The most widespread and devastating epidemic began in Constantinople, that bridge between the Eastern and Western worlds, in 1347. During the next two years it swept across Europe; in some countries an estimated one-half or two-thirds of the people died. In England a third, possibly a half, of the population was taken. Severe labor shortage was an immediate result of this disaster. Landowners began to enclose land areas that had been open to public domain, and sheep-raising increased. With the accumulation of capital and large landholdings impressive fortunes were established and political and social systems were irrevocably altered. Thus a disease could have consequences that were as unpremeditated as they were far-reaching.

Again in 1665 London was decimated by the Black Death. It swept across the countryside, particularly afflicting

51

ports and riversides from which ship-borne, flea-carrying rats spread the plague. If the plague originated in the East, it is interesting that initial steps toward its eradication also began there: During a great epidemic in China the plague germ was discovered.

The horrors of the Black Death were rivaled by those of the dread smallpox. The experience of the American Indians, particularly our Southern tribes, might be representative of the ruin this disease wrought for centuries around the world. With smallpox the leading scourge, "the initial damage done to the Southeastern Indians by European diseases was far greater than anything Europeans could have inflicted with weapons and military suppression," one anthropologist has written.

Among the Cherokees smallpox usually meant death because of their belief in curing illness by bathing in running waters. For those few who did recover, the ugliness of a pockmarked skin left spiritual scars as well. Dragging Canoe, the resourceful and implacable enemy of all white people, was pockmarked. The rumor was spread through the tribes that the English sometimes infected their trade wares deliberately to weaken the native owners of the land. Our history has failed to record in sufficient depth the impact of European germs, and the reaction of Indian shamans and medicine-men and folkways, on the early development of our country.

With that relief we may remember the agony of the Black Death and smallpox today. At least two of humankind's oldest and cruelest enemies are no longer with us. This success can encourage us in waging present and future battles.

If you wanted to acquaint strangers in a distant land with this country and its people what single book would you give them to read?

That question was put to a number of readers, teachers, librarians, critics and editors a few years ago when we were reopening a dialogue with China. What book would you send to the Chinese people to tell them about America and Americans?

The answers were varied and interesting. But the book which received nomination most often was Mark Twain's *Huckleberry Finn.*

In many ways this was a surprising selection. Mark Twain was a product of the frontier in many meanings of that word; his parents lived for a while, just before he was born, in the village of Jamestown, Tennessee, not far from the Kentucky line. His two most famous books are considered children's, or young people's books, and he is often put under the category of humorist.

Well, Mark Twain's frontiers were not only along the Mississippi River and in gold camps of the West, they were of human relationships and therefore timeless. And anyone who thinks of him as a children's writer or a folksy yarn-spinner hasn't read his works. He was often most profound when he was simplest, and most bitter when he was laughing.

Everyone has a little of Huck Finn in him — and that is why the story of this honest, ragtag, outlandishly human boy continues to speak to the experience of each successive generation.

Twain's wit, too, was universal. It still pricks and nudges and undermines our pomposity and prejudices today, exploding us out of our hypocrisy and our smugness, blowing like a fresh breeze across our minds.

Perhaps it would be a good spring tonic to partake again of some Mark Twain insights:

"In all matters of opinion, our adversaries are insane."

"Familiarity breeds contempt — and children."

"There is a lot to say in her favor, but the other (things to say) are more interesting."

"If you pick up a starving dog and make him prosperous, he will not bite you. This is the principal difference between a dog and a man."

"Everyone is a moon and has a dark side which he never shows to anybody."

"Wagner's music is better than it sounds."

"A boy is hounded to death and robbed of his natural rest because Ben Franklin said once, in one of his inspired flights of malignity: 'Early to bed and early to rise — Makes a man healthy, wealthy and wise." As if it were any object to a boy to be healthy and wealthy and wise on such terms."

"Within the last generation each Christian power has turned the bulk of its attention to finding out newer and still newer and more effective ways of killing Christians, and, incidentally, a pagan now and then; and the surest way to get rich quickly in Christ's earthly kingdom is to invent a gun that can kill more Christians at one shot than any other existing kind."

"You can't pray a lie," Huck Finn - Mark Twain says. And he hated people who tried to live lies. He laughed — and wept.

IT IS an illness which many people do not consider an illness at all.

And yet . . . it can cause a man to give up his work, a woman to forget her duty, and children to commit foolish and even dangerous acts.

It may commence with a sound (the clip-clop of horse's hooves on cobbled street in a French town, as Thomas Wolfe described it), or a taste (the flavor of homemade bread, or cider dripping from a wooden press), or a smell (lilacs on a spring afternoon, or sea wind blowing fresh from the ocean), or a sight (view from a familiar hilltop, glimpse of a forgotten toy or trophy) . . .

It may begin in the throat or the stomach, with a tightening, a seizure, a wrench that seems to cut off swallowing and hinder breathing, and then it spreads to the rest of the body in a languishing of tone and spirit.

It is the affliction known as homesickness.

And if you are so sophisticated that you have never experienced it, or if you are so inflexible that you do not wish to admit its experience, then perhaps part of the reason lies in your lack of knowledge of what a "home" can mean.

Of course, we are not speaking of the sort of home that is a sort of prison, holding its members in invisible bonds of miplaced love and misguided protectiveness. Part of the purpose of a home is to build the strength that will make it possible to leave — and return at will. But given any human sensitivity there are moments when memories of home rush in with such vividness and vigor that for a moment we know

55

what is meant by the term — homesickness.

In fact, I discovered it recently in an old doctor book. The passage intrigued me: "Nostalgia. Homesickness, especially a sufficient degree of it to cause mental and bodily depression, is called nostalgia. It may amount to a serious disability. For example, when the youthful Louis Pasteur first left his father's tannery in the village of Arbois to study at Paris, he was attacked by nostalgia to such an extent that he became visibly ill. He confessed to one of his companions, 'If only I could get a whiff of the tannery yard, I feel I would be cured.' His condition grew so alarming that his father was summoned, and took him home. Thus the boy smelled the beloved tannery once more, and was restored to his family and to peace."

Knowing that the great Pasteur suffered from nostalgia might comfort many families who have a fledgling in the world for the first time — "away" at school, at summer camp, in service, on a first job, visiting far afield.

For my own part, I recall a struggle with nostalgia when I was a child more vividly than several subsequent illnesses requiring hospitalization. But it is the only one I cherish — and would not forego if time repeated itself.

WHEN THE sharp cold of winter closes in, a new mood descends on nature and a new mode of life begins.

The wind changes. Breezes that were soft and benign bear a sudden bite — and windows thrown open early in the nighttime are lowered to small cracks before the morning light. Any stirring of air penetrates clothing and shelter and reminds us of the need for thickness and tightness and sturdy workmanship.

The sunlight alters. More welcome than ever, it has nevertheless relinquished part of its dominance over the days and wherever it spreads its fingers of light the brilliance is thin and the warmth is token. Because of its sparseness perhaps it is more welcome than ever!

The trees are different. Stripped of gentle foliage they appear bare before the snows and storms that will attack them during coming months. It is difficult to discern which twigs and limbs are dead and which still live, awaiting only the rising sap of another spring.

Even the streams are not the same. Their waters seem to glisten with brighter reflections. Their pace seems more sharp and hurried. The pebbles on their beds shine with many varied hues of color and light. And in deep pools under overhanging rhododendron clumps the brooks seem dark and cold and secret in their momentary stillness and hiding.

Indeed, it is a time of changing mood and mode.

Yet it is a good time.

There is a sense of challenge in the air. There is an awareness of fundamentals. Heat and clothing and shelter assert first call to our attention. Whether our responses and surroundings are elaborate and luxurious, or sparse and minimal — or in between — the human society must adjust to nature's season. We must know anew that we are only one part of a great design.

Also, this is a time for snugness, for something we might call "innerness." Rooms that were merely passageways or momentary stopovers during the summer are now our modern caves, offering us sanctuary, bringing us together. The first winter fire in the fireplace heralds that feeling of comfort and deep satisfaction that can come only from watching and feeling live flames in the chimney and live coals on the hearth. The first hard freeze outdoors turns us

57

to the harvest indoors, to books, music and conversation, with whetted appetites and thankfulness.

A sense of coziness fills rooms with draperies drawn against the night and cold. Coziness makes breakfast welcome and evening good. Our innermost selves are now our world.

The hour was very late and the night was very dark. Neighbors' lights had disappeared and there seemed to be no existence beyond the windows and walls of my own sheltering cocoon.

Then I opened the door to enjoy a great gulp of fresh air — and I was transported into another world. An active, swirling, almost violent world surrounded the quiet, unlit houses, and a new, mysterious presence was coming among us.

Snow.

The white flakes fell thickly, wedding sky to earth in a close relationship, reminder of the old saying that when there is a heavy white fall like this, the old woman in the clouds is plucking her geese. Indeed, the air seemed as soft and the ground as cushioned as if filled with luxurious down.

With the bustle of daytime noises stifled, the rustle of nature's sounds emerged. The whisper of the snow against fallen leaves and dead limbs bespoke the gentle, inevitable arrival of winter. The occasional fierce whiplash of wind whistling among the flakes and around the house corners warned of the invincible force of winter. Such voices reach deep into our subconscious, awakening memories of murky caves lit by golden firelight, the ancient yearning for shelter and safety and a sense of coziness, snugness against the wet and chill.

The smell of the snow lay along the wind, too; no scent more delicate, more subtle than this blend of freshness as if drawn from watery deeps and fragrance such as that yielded by trailing arbutus and other earliest wildflowers of the spring.

By morning it was sufficient to transform the landscape. And as I think each autumn that I will store up memories of the woods in all their flaming or subdued richness of colors, so each winter I am sure that I will remember how snow looks upon earth and town, woods and fields, clustered houses and distant mountain ranges. But each year the vividness of October and the whiteness of December come again to reveal how inadequate the memory is when confronted with the reality of experience.

Looking out upon the new world, going out to participate in its routines, the staccato schedules of humans or the more sustained rhythms of nature, the knowledge is reasserted of snow's revelations and concealments. The pure crystalline blanket hides accumulations of debris and waste and ugliness. It softens sharp edges and bandages scars of roadsides and uninhabited buildings.

Snow's revelations are as tiny as the tracery of a bird track on the windowsill and as majestic as the sculpted slope of a pinnacle on the distant horizon. The scrawled blackness of an elm branch becomes a masterpiece of design outlined with a frosting of snow.

As a surprise, it came in the night. As a delight it accumulated in the morning. First snow. Winter has left us its annual calling card.

AT THIS SEASON many features of our mountain landscape that do not attract our attention in the lavish richness of summer and autumn come more clearly into our vision. A path that is hidden under a canopy of trees is suddenly evident as the cover is stripped away and the meandering trail is revealed.

Rocks and boulders that were recently softened by luxuriant surroundings of shrubs and woods emerge in their stark, immobile grandeur. Contours of hills and valleys stand boldly forth in the clear sharp air of winter.

So, too, does the modest galax plant come into its glory now. Lustrous green or burnished bronze, glistening in the sun, polished by snow and rain, it creates pockets of beauty on many a hillside, near many a stream.

During the years of the Great Depression, I recall most vividly seeing children my age, or even smaller, standing on the streets of Asheville selling clusters of galax leaves tied with bits of string, carried sometimes in a homemade basket of white oak or honeysuckle. They stood in the corners and offered their harvest from the woods with tentative gestures and bleak little smiles, and I shall never forget this sight.

The name of "galax" comes from the Greek word meaning "milk." This is from the same language root as galaxy, the astronomer's name for the Milky Way. It has been said that this little plant is about as near stemless as a plant can be, but its leaves, roundish-heart-shaped, with points around the edge conspicuously veined, are borne on long petioles which rise from the ground. The leaves are naturally so well protected against drying out that even after they are picked they remain fresh and green for a long time. It is this quality, plus the fact that the petioles are so stiff that wires are not needed to hold them in place, which has made galax a favorite wreath and decorative green. It was introduced into the florist's trade in 1890.

For years this small plant provided many mountain families with supplementary income, and sometimes it wasn't only supplementary, it was essential.

In December 1921 a reporter published the following observations on the subject: "It is not perhaps generally known that the galax industry in the mountains is one upon which several hundred families are dependent, and the pursuit of which is highly encouraged by officials of the U.S. Forestry Service. Galax and forest fires cannot inhabit the same territory; in other words the galax pickers are the best of volunteer forest rangers, quick to spot the dread flames that spell an end to their livelihood and industrious in stamping out the conflagration while it is yet possible to control it. New York and Philadelphia are the main markets for these leaves."

Long may galax flourish in our hills and valleys!

WHO OWNS this place where I live.

Oh, I have legal title to it. My name is duly recorded on a deed duly registered in the processes of human commerce and law. But this is only one kind of possession. Perhaps it is the least important possession.

Consider the other inhabitants on my acres.

There are the cardinals that winter here, appear at my

feeding station, build nests in the spring, dart with flashes of scarlet brilliance through the greenery of summer or the white snows of winter. They are worried by no boundary lines designating ownership.

There are the mocking birds that seek out the highest limbs from which to pour forth their liquid dazzling variety of songs and calls, and the plump mourning doves that run along the ground or wing on short flights from one low tree limb to another. There are the robins that enliven my lawn with their neat, attentive presence, and the starlings that roar in periodically — scrounging and greedy. They await no invitation to visit or inhabit this place that must be designated "ours."

There are the insects that inhabit every inch of surface here, even though I encounter them only occasionally. They whirl out of the grasses as I walk across the yard, they zoom out of bushes along the driveway, and they throng in the garden — vegetables or flowers — I try to cultivate. Their numbers awe me. (I understand the scientific theory that this may be called the age of the insects.) Their variety interests me. (They range from the pure destructiveness of the Japanese beetles to the sophisticated society and usefulness of the bees.) Their noises fill the day — and night. (Is there a sound more ripe with the essence of late summer than the cries of the katy-dids in the early velvet darkness?)

There are the small animals that lurk in hidden shadows and know my routes of passage and my routines of work better than I know theirs. Occasionally at night my headlights catch the darting form of a sprightly rabbit. Once, quite a while ago, a possum sought refuge under shrubs a distance behind our house. One rainy evening late in the spring I smelled a skunk; it must have been prowling over alien territory for it never reappeared. Even in the middle of town, woods and the bluff that leads to the river in front

62

of my house provide habitat for these little creatures—and for the squirrels that are my favorites. Bushy tails flipping to and fro, alert to every sound and movement, they inhabit totally: Saving their winter's food from oaks and hickories and Chinese chestnuts; storing their loot in the ground, in nooks and crannies; exploring crevices and holes as well as sources of food.

There is all the variety of life that owns the giant oak and elm and maple in my yard. These trees are veritable apartment houses of inhabitants ranging from borers beneath their covers of bark to the shy owl that visits late at night and utters its mysterious cry.

The psychologist, William James, once said, "The instinct of ownership is fundamental in man's nature." I enjoy "my" acres. But I also remember that Thoreau observed, "The highest law gives a thing to him who can use it." And I know that use makes several owners of this place.

ARE YOU a thinger or a thinker?

There are, of course, people who are both. Some of the profound or original thinkers of the world, a few of those we know who give first priority to the life of thought and honing their intellect, are also among the people who enjoy possessions of varying value and quantity.

But for the most part, there is a rather clear division between those in the world who hunger to possess and those who thirst to know.

Several years ago my husband and I became acquainted with a brilliant lady who had retired from an active and creative career to "settle down" in Tryon, N.C. The house where she lived and received a constant flow of fascinating guests was small and unassuming. Nestled in a wooded area, its spacious porch and living room, tiny kitchen and bedrooms, were furnished simply. There was no array of period pieces, imported valuables, priceless ornaments. But on her walls were detailed maps of various areas of the world. Pins of various colors served as a code to impart instant information about specific wars or situations or people. Books lined the walls and lay on window seat and table like old friends ready to be turned to at a moment's whim. And when this bright-eyed, quick-witted lady began to talk, the walls of the house expanded to embrace another world; our minds and interests stretched to horizons we had not glimpsed before.

"I can't give all my energy and attention to minding a big house and elaborate furnishings," she said as she welcomed us.

But she shared with us something more rare: A big mind and elaborately furnished memories of worldwide interest.

Not long ago, my husband and I were on a trip and accepted an invitation to have dinner with a man who is widely known for his collection of rare books, handsome furniture, and unusual autographs. It was a pleasant evening, satisfying to the eye and palate and sense of discreet comfort. As we examined some of the beautifully bound books, some of the unique volumes and autographs, there was no discussion of the content of the pages, or the person who was behind the signature. All attention was focused on the object itself; ideas, passion, communication were secondary to the possession of a physical object.

The need to have; the need to know: Each can shape our life.

An English writer has said, "Possession means to sit astride of the world, instead of having it astride of you." On the other hand, Cicero summed up his belief succinctly:

64

"To think is to live." Possessions sometimes burden us; thinking gives wings to our truest selves.

This does not mean that people who possess things do not also think. But it is the extension of thought — beyond daily needs and grasps into larger realms — an enlargement of the world of self, that we refer to here.

Squirrels can hoard — acorns and hickory nuts and all manner of mast. Birds can accumulate — twigs and leaves and all sorts of materials for a worthy nest. Humans, too, can hoard and accumulate — but they can also think! As the wise Frenchman, Pascal, observed, "Man is but a reed, the most feeble thing in nature, but he is a thinking reed."

Am I basically a thinger or a thinker?

Perhaps like many people I am torn between the two. I delight in things that are beautiful and useful and unique. I could spend a lifetime gathering, polishing, enjoying. But I also agree with doughty old Sam Johnson: "All knowledge is of itself some value. There is nothing so minute or inconsiderable that I would not rather know it than not." And I would rather spend a lifetime in that realm.

Are you a thinger or a thinker? It's a tantalizing question, involving daily choices.

COLD LOCKS the ground in a frozen grip.

Snow and sleet alternate with pale sunlight to mark the gradually lengthening days.

Thermometers fall to reach new lows for the year and everything seems in hiding from the icy grip of winter.

But the seed catalogues arrive.

There they are, sprawled before us in rare perfection,

those juicy red tomatoes, crisp green cucumbers, plump golden corn, succulent squashes and tender beans, in all their summer abundance. Winter vanishes before these visions of the warm earth and sprouting seeds to come.

As the bulletins and catalogues from nurseries and seed firms rekindle plans for spring, I recall that we are all — even the most remote and isolated among us — internationalists when it comes to our gardens. Without exchanges between past civilizations how limited and barren our gardens might be today!

Man first lived by wild meats, grains, fruits, bulbs, roots and herbs. Then, probably more than 20,000 years ago, he began to cultivate certain plants. Historians assure us that such bulbs as the tulip, hyacinth, and narcissus were considered equally as edible and nutritious as the onion and garlic. And in Mexico, before the coming of maize (Indian corn), which occurred in prehistoric times, the dahlia was an important source of starchy food. As for potatoes, now a common source of starch in Mexico, they were probably brought to that country from South America by the Spanish explorers and adventurers.

Thus, over the years, plants have changed their purposes and habitat. It has taken all mankind to create our present gardens.

For instance, we have probably never credited the Indian fully enough for all that he has given us. One authority says: "The American Indians were the world's most successful cultivators of domesticated plants. No less than half of the plants in cultivation today are Indian discoveries, among them maize, America's most important, and the world's second most important, foodstuff. The potato, too, Europe's chief food plant, as well as beans, cocoa, tobacco, tomatoes, gourds, quinine, vanilla, and many others, originate from the New World."

66

Thumbing through seed advertisements, planning next season's garden, it is exciting to consider how old a tradition we follow and how indebted we are to the "savages" who preceded us on this continent.

Perhaps as we plant our seeds we might remember that, for the most part, they treated this earth and its wealth of fertility, wild creatures, clear waters, its unpoisoned air and mysterious brooding silence, with more respect than our "civilization" has shown. "As ye sow, so shall ye reap."

An outstanding teacher came to see me recently. Her age may have been the 65 years she claimed, but her appearance and vitality suggested a woman closer to 45. When I asked her what she would consider an essential ingredient or talent for a successful teacher, she immediately replied, "A sense of humor!"

Her reply delighted me, for I believe that a sense of humor is necessary for any successful life — if by a successful life we mean that experience which brings some sense of fulfillment, some inner harmony which reaches into the outer world and touches other lives as well. Humor provides perspective. Humor diminishes our ego while it nourishes our shared humanity. Humor allows us to be serious about the significant aspects of our life without being grim about the trivia. It makes us delightful associates for family and friends.

There are many kinds of humor, of course. Perhaps the one line quip, the wisecrack that characterizes our present source of laughter, suggests some of the loss in our contemporary life. There was a time when our country, and especially this region of our country, was distinguished by the folk yarn, the tall tale, the personal anecdote that was exchanged during long afternoons and leisurely evenings when people still visited one another and talked in flavorful, individualistic language.

Recall some of those moments:

Remember Oaty, a prototype of the spinner of yarns who "would rather climb a tree and tell a lie than stay on the ground and tell the truth." When she was asked about his unique brand of truth, his wife was philosophic: "He only lies enough to enjoy himself."

And there were the political humorists, including North Carolina's Civil War Governor Zeb Vance and Tennessee's Davy Crockett, of whom Governor Bob Taylor was king. Listeners never forget his way with an anecdote. "I saw the school commissioners visit the 'old field' school teacher, and heard them question him as to his system of teaching. They asked him whether, in geography, he taught that the world was round or that the world was flat. With great dignity he replied: "That depends upon whar I'm teachin'. If my patrons desire me to teach the round system, I teach that; and if they desire me to teach the flat system, I teach that." Or: "An old Texan once told me the Texas climate was the quickest climate in the world. He said that an old farmer was driving along one day; his team was composed of oxen; and it was so hot that one of the oxen fell dead from sunstroke, and, while he was skinning him, the other one froze to death."

Exaggeration was basic to the tall tale. "I've seen it so hot till all the stumps and logs on a 10-acre clearing crawled off in the shade and cleared up the new ground." Or, "The tallest man I ever saw was getting a haircut in heaven and a shoeshine in hell."

One Southern editor used to tell the story of the Arkansas farmer who was urged by a book agent to purchase a set of books on scientific agriculture. "If you had these books you could farm twice as good as you do." The old fellow looked at the salesman. "Heck, son, I don't farm half as good as I know how now."

It is good to recall some of the easygoing, unsophisticated humor that has carried our region through depressions and disasters. As my teacher-friend observed, it's an important element of our lives.

Perhaps it is no accident that running has become a way of life for us. (We even "run" for public office.) Running suggests goals, stamina, a need for haste to turn to other accomplishments. Walking, on the other hand, invites exploration of the surrounding landscape, contemplation, perhaps even a nod to a neighbor or a stranger. And doctors assure us that walking is "one of the best — if not the best — exercises for the entire body."

The very simplicity of walking probably makes it suspect in our society. No special costume is necessary. No accompanying music is required. No best selling books of directions are called for. Who can promote such an undertaking?

People in touch with themselves, with their minds and spirits as well as their muscles, reap the rewards of walking. A doctor has pointed out that "Beethoven composed best while walking after eating. Goethe walked a lot. Einstein puzzled out many secrets of the universe on his walks around Princeton. Mark Twain was a pacer."

All my life I have lived with people who were practiced in the art of walking. My father brought a real sense of occasion to a walk in the woods. He would select a cane from the fascinating collection he kept beside our front door — not because he needed a cane for support or protection but because he felt that every walker should have a stick to poke among leaves or prod interesting stones or point to particular vistas. Sometimes he would talk and sometimes he would be silent. Either way there was a deep sense of communication with the earth and with anyone walking with him.

My mother has always believed that a walker should move briskly, "to get the circulation going." At home she runs up and down two flights of stairs countless times each day. She walks around yard and pool and flower beds breaking off dead weeds, picking up stray sticks, just for relaxation. She's been up in the Rockies and down in the Grand Canyon and on a morning walk in Norway once she would have put a Viking to shame. She likes to feel earth beneath her feet.

My husband shaped much of the course of his life by walking. On a walk long ago he decided to buy some woodland which signified that he would not enter the business career he had planned. Pursuing some special studies at Princeton he encountered, on several occasions, Einstein on his solitary walks. Whether James "puzzled out many secrets of the universe" on his own walks I couldn't say. But it reassured him to discover that walking was an integral part of Einstein's life and thought, and could add depth and meaning to anyone's experience.

Recently my two sons have walked: one along paths in Australia, Nepal, Kenya; the other in remote regions of China among people whose only transportation is afoot.

Beethoven. Mark Twain. Parents. Husband. Children. Who am I not to follow such examples?

IMAGINE THAT YOU are in the woods, deep in the wilderness, with only the sounds of wind and water and perhaps leaves overhead or underfoot, and the rustling noises of small animals, birds, insects, carrying forward their hidden lives all around you; and there, suddenly, in the sun-splattered shade you see an animal you had never expected to see.

The stranger stands alert and proud, its thick shiny fur ranging from silver shades of grey through beige streaks into brown. Its pointed face is framed between two pointed ears which emphasize the keenness of the watchful eyes. In size it may range from 50 or 60 pounds to 110 or 120, depending on age, and except for its feet, which are the most immediately apparent difference, it might be a large German shepherd dog. The feet are large, with a wide spread at every well-padded step the graceful animal takes. You are facing a timber wolf.

What would your first reaction be?

Judging by the past, the most common reaction would be to kill it. That is why it is one of the world's endangered species today.

Our reason for our unreasonable fear of the wolf is the historical cloud of myth and legend surrounding its presence and habits. In childhood we read about Little Red Riding Hood and the trouble she and her grandmother had with a wolf. We hear about Peter and the Wolf (who was much more interesting than some of his friends, the duck and cat and others), as well as the shepherd boy who cried "wolf" once too often. Later, the horror fantasies of the werewolf grip our imagination. And throughout our lives we are surrounded by conversational slights against this animal's character: It is unattractive to wolf down food, it is depressing to find the wolf at the door and it is a vain and fickle lover who is a wolf.

In reality, the wolf deserves none of these demerits. I was introduced to a wolf by the son of a friend of mine, a tall, lean, articulate young man who looks at once like a scholar and an outdoorsman.

David owns(?) Ida, a 6-month-old wolf. She was born in captivity, but in reality she is a wild animal — watchful, hyperactive, at once tense and relaxed, enormously handsome. In response to the myths about wolves, David points out that they mate for their entire lives (more faithful than human "wolves"), that they live by an established social order and they don't kill for fun — only for food (less savage than many human predators). David also repeats a fact which has received attention only recently: That there is "no instance" in our history of North America of a healthy wild wolf attacking a man.

Perhaps the wolf knows instinctively how much it has to fear from man. On all of this continent there are probably only about 6000 wolves remaining in the wild. Bounty hunting is still encouraged in some places. Anyone who has seen photographs of hunting by snowmobile or plane knows what a thoroughly inhumane, shamefully unsportsmanlike, pastime it is.

David's travels with Ida are not intended to encourage use of wild animals as pets ("bad things happen to 80 or 90 per cent of the people who have wolves as pets"), but to dramatize the proud and irreplaceable wildlife we are destroying. It is an urgent message.

There are those who consider writing (or reading) a novel an escape from reality.

Certain novels are written for precisely that purpose, of course, just as certain foods are manufactured to satisfy a momentary hunger rather than provide permanent nourishment. But I am not referring to junk food novels. I'm speaking of those that probe to the quick of life. They stir us to laughter, rage, pity, horror, renewed awareness of the human condition — and they put us into closer touch with "reality" than tons of statistics, reams of "facts."

Consider how much of our knowledge of other times and places comes not from bureaucratic reports but from the individual vision of novelists whose works have endured to our own time. And what, I wonder, will future generations say about our world today as reflected in its novels, in its fiction that is dispensed daily, nightly, hourly into millions of homes via that magic screen?

Even more important, perhaps, what does this so-called fiction tell us about ourselves: our values, our fears, our hopes, our apathy, our compassion?

A few days ago I finished at least the first draft of a long and demanding effort to recreate a segment of life during a crucial period of history in our country. And almost simultaneously I came upon a statement written by Edith Hamilton, renowned as a scholar and celebrator of the ancient classical world. She addressed the subject which lies at the heart of our vision of ourselves, unless we are to yield totally to the commercialism which exploits and titillates, providing a distorted, crippled view of life. There is another problem, too.

But let Edith Hamilton say it so much better:

"'I detest nature,' Picasso has said. He is the spokesman for the art of our age, for the music we are listening to, the pictures we are looking at, the books we are reading. Today the usual and the normal, which is to say the natural, is being discarded. What is called abstract art has taken a foremost place . . .

"Our artists are escaping from reality. This is no new thing, to be sure. In almost all ages there have been artists who escaped. What is new in our age is the direction they are taking. In the past a detestation of nature led persistently to the land of heart's desire where everyone and everything was good and true and beautiful. Now it leads to just the opposite, where nothing is good or true or beautiful. Of course one is just as much an escape as the other. It is just as far from reality to shut out all that is agreeable as to shut out all that is disagreeable. Both extremes are equally unreal, and both are equally romantic.

"Romance is the refusal to accept things as they are. All art bears either the romantic stamp or the classic. To the classic artist his chosen field is things as they are. He is repelled by anything unfamiliar and extraordinary and he detests extremes. The Greeks had no desire to turn away from nature. They did not see the usual and the normal as commonplace. The way they looked at them is perfectly exemplified in the statue of a girl bending over a basin to wash her hands. She is classic art in herself; beauty is embodied in a completely ordinary act. The Greeks saw beauty and significance in nature."

Both ways of interpreting the world have their dangers, of course: one may put form above spirit; the other may be-

74

come sentimental. It is the sentimentality of unrelieved brutality that threatens much of our vision today. Our novels, our televised fiction, must return to the reality of nature seen whole as we explore inner as well as outer space.

PERHAPS ONE WAY to define personality — our own or another person's — is to discover the season we carry within us.

Don't you know people who live as though life were one long summer? Without the fever of youth or the fret of age, they seek to stay suspended in the blissful warmth between any extremes. They agree with Napoleon when he said, "Were I to choose a religion, I would probably become a worshiper of the sun." Those with summertime attitudes and beliefs seek the leisure and relaxation of arrival: Safety, certainty, the sun in its heaven and all's right with the world.

Then there are those who are autumn characters. They are forever directed toward the harvest. Riches of goods and friendship may be theirs, but it is the accumulation rather than the experience of these treasures that is made paramount. It is a worthy season; the poet Shelley wrote, "There is a harmony in Autumn, and a lustre in its sky . . ." So those who carry fall within may also have found harmony in abundance — or a millstone.

And what of the ones who shape their lives by the winter within them? It is a closed season, a time of buried seeds and fastened doors and draped windows, when man and nature turn inward — toward bitter withdrawal or beneficent renewal. Shakespeare spoke of winter taming "man, woman and beast," and said, "a safe tale's best for winter." There are those who live as if they carried the tameness and sadness of many winters through each day's new-minted hours.

Last — first, best, most welcome — there are people we know who harbor springtime and share its energy throughout their lives. They see each morning afresh. They welcome new beginnings. Their beauty does not flow from any sentimental prettiness but from deep reservoirs of affirmation and faith. When they are young they are not afraid to anticipate and dream and spend enthusiasm; when they are older they are not defeated by autumn's disappointments or winter's treats. They know that man, no less than nature, is born for many resurrections.

This is the day for those who know that spring is the season for courage, the courage to hope; for strength, the strength to discover that joy is possible. Easter is the interval for renewal. To keep it green throughout the other seasons of our life, we must tap the deepest wellsprings of our creation.

EVERYONE HAS personal reminders by which the arrival of spring is heralded. No matter what the red line on the thermometer indicates, no matter whether there are still pockets of snow in the mountains or patches of ice on ponds, the harbinger announces that spring is lurking in the wings, ready to come onstage in a few hours ... or days ... or even weeks.

One of the earliest signals of spring that stirs my spirit and lifts my hope is the sound of the "peepers," or frogs, in hidden pools or puddles of water that were often not even apparent until the shrill cries of their small inhabitants affirmed that there was dampness there.

When I was a child I heard this chorus of spring each year at the pool just beyond by bedroom window. It was a wide shallow pool fed by a natural spring, surrounded by rhododendron and ferns, galax and many wild flowers that my parents had nurtured there. On summer days it was a haven of clear, cool beauty. In winter it was a sparkling reflection of freeze or thaw. But in spring it became the nursery and the symbol of all the life that would soon be bursting forth from the earth.

Occasionally I would awaken during one of those spring evenings. Warm sweet winds would be blowing gently through the open windows. The darkness would not seem threatening but rich and kind, folding the world in a sense of mystery. And outside, from the living, breathing world of plants and creatures whose lives and passages were largely unknown to me, came the chorus of the peepers. It was a call at once wild and familiar stirring the imagination. I have felt similar responses in faraway places: At the Sacred Well in the ancient Mayan city of Chichen Itza in Yucatan, where I sat one evening undisturbed and heard birds cry in the surrounding jungle; at the sacred temple in the Greek ruins at Delphi, where wind sighed down from the surrounding pinnacles and wrapped the place and the moment in loneliness and wonder.

For many people spring is not a sound but a sight. Crocus in bloom are many people's tocsin that the change of seasons has arrived. Bright splashes of purple and yellow, even in snow, are rejuvenating to the spirit. But the crocus has one short-coming: Its lack of odor.

Perhaps that is why the shrub we call breath-of-spring is a more distinct signal of spring for me. Its sprawling branches may appear brown and dormant, its blossoms are small and modest, not significantly colorful in their white and creamy shades — but they fill the air with a fragrance that is as fresh as the March wind itself — and much less demanding of attention.

Last year I was compelled to prune severely some of the aging breath-of-spring bushes scattered around our yard. Their young sprouts seem healthy and abundant. But they have not yet provided that perfume we had come to expect as part of spring's arrival. Perhaps next year . . . Meanwhile, I'll listen for the peepers in their hidden pools. Welcome spring.

BENEATH A sheltering rhododendron bush, beside a clear spring-fed pool, near a winding stream — at three different places around my mother's home near Asheville — the shortia is in bloom once more.

Shortia is one of our mountain plants so delicate and rare that not many natives and few strangers in Southern Appalachia have ever seen it. Like many of our people, it does not adapt well to transplantation. Like much of our history, its story is little known. A few years ago I gathered details of its initial discovery and loss by a European botanist. This season of its bloom seems an appropriate time for calling attention to its discovery — and rediscovery — even as this region and its people are "rediscovered" from time to time.

Shortia is a small perennial that grows close to the ground in damp, rich earth. Its glossy leaves bespeak its kinship to the larger galax. Its pure white flowers have five fringed petals and their bell shape has given them their popular name, "oconee bells."

One of the rarest flowers in our mountains, shortia is found in only a few counties in North and South Carolina and Georgia. Indeed, it was so infrequently encountered that for several generations it was known as the lost plant of the Southern Appalachians.

The French botanist, Andre Michaux, discovered shortia during his travels in the Blue Ridge in the 1780s. The eminent naturalist, Donald Culross Peattie, has described Michaux as he must have looked when he returned to the port of Charleston after one of his long expeditions into the unmapped wilderness: "At the head of a pack train laden down with hundreds of plants — packets of seeds, frail flowers in moss, and shrubs and young trees balled in earth, swaying and joggling to the gate of the garden, looking bewildered and unnatural in this lowland heat and glare."

As he took his specimens back to Europe, Michaux's colleagues studied and named each one. With a single exception. One little leaf and pod — a mere fragment — had no notation except that it was found "in the high mountains of Carolina."

Half a century passed. Then Dr. Asa Gray and John Torrey were in Paris preparing the monumental work, *A Flora of North America,* and they discovered Michaux's little plant. Declaring it a new genus they named shortia in honor of Dr. Charles Wilkins Short, a pioneer botanist of Kentucky.

As soon as he returned to America, in summer of 1840, Dr. Gray began a search for "the little shrub with scalloped leaves." For years he hunted in vain. At last he wrote, "I grew sorrowful at having named after Dr. Short a plant that nobody could find."

It was Charles Sprague Sargent of Massachusetts, who finally turned back to Michaux's original diary and sought out the wild and beautiful country of the Toxaway River.

In the autumn of 1886, almost a century after its first discovery, shortia was rediscovered — in a region of "steep
gabled high ridges drenched much of the time in rains, its
plunging stream valleys prepetually shaded by dense rhododendron thickets."

A century later Peattie wrote of his own first sight of
shortia. Walking through the heavy forest under a veil of rain
"suddenly, right under my feet, spreading far as I could see
under the rhododendron, growing on the steep bank, I beheld the long-sought-for little flower, its frail sweet bells
swinging under the first pelting of rain."

No wonder my mother cherishes the plants brought to
her years ago by a friend, plants that responded to her
careful nurturing.

BEVERLY HILLS was living up to its legend.

Early morning sun slanted through the tall windows of
our bedroom. Outside the brilliant green of trees and shrubs
and deep-piled carpets of grass turned the world into a tropical paradise.

Below one of our windows a gardener on his knees manicured the edges of the walk winding from the driveway to
the wide front entrance. Occasionally he diverted his attention to a clump of flowers from which he pulled a random
weed with all the care of a dentist extracting a worrisome
tooth.

Birds brought the sound of music to the morning. It was
the only sound in the 9 o'clock stillness. At home, 9 o'clock

is midmorning, but in Beverly Hills it is just past midnight. We were visiting friends and the wife is an actress. After a late night's work we could understand why she needed sleep. But we were wide awake and so we tiptoed downstairs, through the expanses of our friend's rented residence.

"I'm going to steal an apple and an orange from the refrigerator and take a walk up the canyon," James decided.

Left alone, I found a cup of coffee (someone had plugged in an early percolator) and a glass of juice and went out to sit by the swimming pool and imagine all the people who had moved in and out of this house in its extensive, expensive past. How luscious the life here seemed. Only a few minutes away were the busy streets where careers and commerce are carried on. From time to time the smog that afflicts Los Angeles might even reach up into these high, exclusive Hollywood hills. But surrounding this enclave were other beautiful homes of the famous and infamous, where the appearance was of water and sun, wealth and serenity. Peace.

At a late lunch we assembled on the patio — our hosts, my wandering husband, and I. When our hostess heard that James had been for a morning stroll she gasped in alarm.

"But you're not supposed to walk in the canyon here — unless you're walking a dog. The police pick up any stranger."

My Tennessee hiker grinned. "I began to be aware of the general atmosphere after a half-dozen places I passed had dogs which sounded alarms and several motorists gave me wary looks."

It seemed incredible to me that people could not readily walk among these green, flower-decked hills, up this luxuriant canyon, at will. "No," our host shook his head. "A friend of ours who is British brought his mother over for a visit

81

and she liked to have her English jaunt around the block each day. She was stopped twice by the police — almost taken to the station."

Later that day we went to see other old friends. After running the gamut of two men at the entrance, a sleek German Police dog, a wary maid and a defensive housekeeper, we almost wondered if it was worth the effort.

Fear occupies the Hollywood hills.

Was this the kind of life that the violence commission reports warned us about? Are we creating a world where our homes will be pampered islands behind barricades which try to shut out the restless, reaching, world around us? God forbid! Let us consider the society we are creating, or permitting. What does it matter if we gain a world of swimming pools and sleek cars and elegant possessions, and lose our freedom to walk, to look at earth and sky, to talk with strangers, to abandon fear?

THREE JAPANESE magnolia trees in our yard put forth their early buds. One, almost white when it is in bloom, held pale petals up on its stiff branches. Another, which has pink blossoms, was a blush of spring against the brown bare twigs surrounding it. The third, a deep rose shade, was a hint of summer riches to come.

Since these, along with the golden showers of forsythia and jonquils, are the earliest flowers we have in any quantity, they are always welcome, always anticipated. Reappearance of their colorful buds — even before the leaves on the limbs around them have begun to show green — is like renewal of a pledge. It is a forerunner of the revival of earth all around us.

Then came the snow.

We looked out in the morning to wind and freeze and swirling snow. And the magnolia buds, some almost open, some still tightly curled, were no longer white and pink and rose. They were the color of coffee. Overnight they had been blighted.

More often than not, this is the fate of our Japanese magnolias. The very quality which makes them so rare, so choice, so prized — their early appearance, defiant of winter — is also an attribute which leaves them prey to sudden injury. It is as if their beauty is also their burden.

Looking at the magnolias withered beneath the layer of late snow, I thought of some of the boys and girls I have watched over the years. I thought of the pressures which fill the world around us, pressures determined to make young people old before they have known youth, to make them smart before they have become wise.

There are all the innocent eyes, the fresh lips and minds, the unblemished skins and hearts, poised at a springtime moment. Within lies a personality to unfold, a character to develop. Only the outermost signs of the potential beauty are visible to our limited sight.

Then, all too often, suddenly there is the frost, the blight. Some old burden left over from our winter's discontent, some knowledge too-soon learned of summer yet to come, has reached out and banished spring's unique blossoming. It can never be recaptured. And, as with the magnolias, how often the fairest, the most cherished, are earliest maimed. Pushed to bloom too early, they become too soon old, sophisticated before they achieve maturity.

83

MARCH IS one of those months, one of those seasons, one of those intervals . . .

before winter has completely loosened its grip and spring has firmly established its hold;

when brown oak leaves are rustling their last dry rattles in the wind and fattening green buds are silently pushing them from their refuge;

in which the frogs raise their insistent cry from hidden swamps and ponds and unsuspected puddles, hoarsely heralding the turn of a season before ice has melted or earth's thaw is permanent;

between raging gales of wind and somnolent hours of sunshine; between the closed and in-drawn coziness of survival and the opening out-reach of new beginnings.

March is a lion and a lamb — not lying down together but cavorting together across open fields and through the streets of sprawling cities.

March is a promise and a threat — drawing forth blooms and then nipping them in the bud.

March is a war-whoop and a lullaby, rushing with destructive fury across the land, whipping waters and trees to frenzy, bowing people before its force, then cradling the earth in gentle warmth and scattering the fragrance of spicewood and hyacinths through the soft air.

March is with us again, March the uninvited visitor, the erratic, indispensable guest.

March resembles people we have known. There is no certainty or constancy with them. For no apparent reason they fluctuate from one mood to another between our encounters with them.

I have such a friend, known since childhood, and it is difficult to maintain friendship with her. We have a lively reunion. Our mutual interests seem so numerous and exciting that I am sure we will always have rapport whenever, wherever we meet. And yet . . . the very next time I see her — which may be in days or years — she may be as formal as a duchess enjoying her protocol, and although we speak we do not say anything to each other. From one conversation to the next I do not know whether we will be laughing and happy or reserved and strained.

All this shifting and accommodating is difficult. It is demanding. Few of us have time or energy to constantly adapt ourselves to the moods of all the people we meet. Friendship is founded, in part, on security. It is the security of knowing that no matter what trifles may intervene, or how long interludes of absence may last, the next meeting will be one of mutual tolerance and good humor.

March offers us little security. March is the relative who arrives without warning and leaves without forethought, laden with luggage that may be packed with goodies or filled with disasters. We welcome the guest, yet there is wariness born of experience in our greeting.

As March either storms its way out, or subsides into April, I salute its departure. It has asked a great deal of us. I hope April is a more constant friend.

A LONG TIME ago I became acquainted with a young man (who eventually became an older man and has since died) who was scholar in the truest sense of the word. He held a responsible position in one of the major oil companies but did not seek the highest executive positions — because "his" time, the hours and days away from his desk, were spent in studies of mathematics, the history of science and enjoyment of music. His pleasure and great wealth was of the mind.

A few years ago I met a retired banker who had moved his residence from the northeast to the Southern Appalachians. He appreicated, indeed he loved, the mountains and on any walk or hike with him he observed each plant and tree, moss and shrub, asking for names, habitat, characteristics. His curiosity was as boundless as his enthusiasm for his adopted place, and I often compared his concern with the apathy shown by many natives who did not know, nor care to know, about the magnificent world around them.

A few days ago I encountered this sentence in a book I was reading: "The purpose of research in every field is to set back the frontier of darkness."

Let us give the word "research" a broad and spacious interpretation. The doctor in his laboratory is pushing back the darkness of sick minds and bodies; the scientist at his calculations is pushing back the shrouds of space; but each of us, as well, when we sharpen our minds, respect the gift of our curiosity, and seek to know more about this world and this adventure called life — we are overcoming our own bit of the darkness.

As an English novelist once said, "I like to understand things because then I can enjoy them. I think knowledge should intensify our pleasures. That is its aim and object, so far as I am concerned."

How right he is! And yet how dreary many of us consider

knowledge to be. Its acquisition is made laborious, when it should be joyous; we plod toward something called learning when we should run and skip and plunge, stumble and rise and run again. Not that research of any kind, and knowledge worthy of the name does not require work. But it is work repaid not only in earning of bread but in winning of our very spirit.

Perhaps we too often mistake facts for knowledge. As an eminent archeologist has pointed out, the kind of unrelated scraps of information one gets on a quiz program offer scant satisfaction. "Bare facts by themselves do not fascinate us; they must be clothed with the play and counterplay which produced them. The defeat of the Spanish Armada in 1588 is a bald historical fact. It takes on meaning when it is shown as the culmination of a play of forces and the clash of the opposing temperaments and philosophies of two nations, personified in the characters of Philip the Second and Elizabeth. To understand these antagonisms, one must know the cultural backgrounds, the ways of thought, and the conflicting traditions of the two peoples. One must study Torquemada and Chaucer, John of Austria and Latimer, the choir stalls of Toledo cathedral and the fan-vaulting of St. George's, Windsor, and even the dances and field sports of the protagonists."

All knowledge then is related. When we know more about the corner of the world where we live, we know more about the green and fragile planet which is home to all humans. Our own little spark of curiosity is a part of the immense mystery which surrounds all life.

To know! To seek to know! How dull and dead we are when we relinquish that right, that rapture in our lives. Whether it is in mathematics or music, woods-knowledge or earth-wisdom, or effort to understand ourselves and those around us — whatever the area of our knowledge, how satisfying to realize that truly "the purpose of research in every field is to set back the frontier of darkness."

Sometimes nature creates a parable, precise as an aspen leaf, playful as an otter. We recently encountered such a parable.

Participants in a Conference on World Affairs assembled at the University of Colorado in Boulder. Representing many countries, professions, and concerns, some sixty men (and a few women) assembled to speak to — and sometimes with — students and to exchange ideas among themselves. Bristling with briefcases, armed with statistics and strategies, rich in achievement and prestige, all arrived.

And then the snow arrived, too.

Without fanfare it came, blowing and erratic at the beginning, then steady and noiseless and ceaseless it continued. The ground vanished. Shrubs disappeared. Small landmarks went into hiding. Gradually, shops and houses and larger buildings lost their identity and became mere shapeless forms, submerged masses in a surrealist landscape. More than three feet of snow altered the landscape — but not the landscape only, a way of life as well.

The automobile became suddenly an asset transformed. Buried under snowbanks, wheels and brakes and accelerators were useless as our human appendix. Those that could be used — with devices to make them manageable on snow and ice — often became impudent and recalcitrant. Mobility, one of the things we cherished most, could no longer be taken for granted.

The people of distinction were reduced (or elevated?),

for one brief interval, to creatures of nature. With the dry cold of a mile-high elevation tingling their faces, with dazzling white snow surrounding their every step and glance, they rearranged airplane schedules, strode to auditoriums and lecture halls, sought out clubs and homes to which they had been invited. Nature's program, for the moment, over-shadowed man's programs.

And above all loomed the mountains.

The Flatirons, those dramatic peaks rising up just above the town of Boulder, are so-called because one side of each of the series of sharp, high mountains is covered with green while the other side is a sheer slice of granite. White and grey, soft and harsh, the Flatirons tower above man's miniature buildings and activities, reserved and silent as the eternities of time which absorb our momentary schedules. Beyond them stretch the higher Rockies, their immensity enough to dwarf the ego of man or nation and challenge each to a more spacious vision.

Nature's parable reminded some World Affairs discussants not to confine our concern to man alone.

ONE OF our kitchen doors opens onto an outdoor patio where we eat many summer meals.

The patio is covered with some sort of tile and has a brick enclosure perhaps four feet high.

A few days ago when I was sweeping an assortment of late-shedding oak leaves, and bits of boxwood, and general dust and debris from the corners, I found a dandelion blooming there.

Between the tiles with their cemented seams, and the

solid bricks and mortar, in some small accumulation of soil, this tiny plant had taken root and thrust up its bright green foliage and its brilliant blossom. It seemed unlikely, out-of-place, and yet curiously appropriate too.

The flower seemed as large as a silver dollar, yet its rich color put one more in mind of a golden coin — perhaps the kind that used to be referred to in adventure novels as Spanish doubloons or Italian ducats. Yet this was a coin from nature's factories, minted by the sun, dropped here perhaps to reassure us that spring was on its way.

I could not bring myself to tear out the so-called weed and sweep it away.

What virtue would there be in my broom uprooting this dandelion, flourishing near our doorway like a plump pincushion, simply to prove I was a tidy housekeeper?

More important, the delicacy and tenderness, the toughness and resilience, of this little plant — choosing to grow in a hostile landscape of brick and tile — carried a message. Its arrogance pleased me. Its meaning gave me pause.

I considered ancient pyramids of long-lost civilizations as I had seen them in Yucatan. Surrounded by jungles, overgrown by tangled vines and shrubs and even trees, many of these mighty works of men stand today buried beneath nature's persistent growth. Those that have been resurrected from their green graves are often crumbled or weakened by the interaction of roots and weather working over the centuries to replace the encroachments of man.

I thought of pictures I had seen of the splendors of Angkor Wat, in Cambodia, where nature's presence broods over the ancient temples that once must have seemed indestructible — yet they are now possessed, at least in part, by stems and trunks and leaves and vines and tentacles.

Perhaps I had best make friends with the dandelion. When the tile and brick which seem to be rejecting it now

90

are long since crumbled, its descendants and relatives may be flourishing on this little plot. And if only one can remain in the long run — the brick or the plant — I hope the green and gold will be survivor.

The warm sun is bathing all the world around me in a light so clear and fresh that distant pinnacles of the Smokies seem almost as close as the hillside just across the river. Birds are busy in the sprawling elm tree and the great old oak just outside my windows. Their runs and trills, their calls and chatter, make the afternoon seem vibrant with life and happiness.

It is a good day. I am filled with satisfaction and pleasure to be home. I am content to contemplate small buds and confront large chores awaiting my attention. When the scent of honeysuckle drifts by with a gust of wind, I try to suck in all the fragrance — thinking how superior is its delicacy and its sweetness to any perfume manufactured by human inventiveness.

It is a good season of the year. In fact, I have welcomed spring at several places and several times during the past months. It is surprising to discover how often spring makes its debut across America.

The first encounter was in Seattle the first of March when I saw a rhododendron in full rosy bloom. The day was invigorating with a robust wind and the scent of rain over Puget Sound and people did not loiter in their walking. Imagine, then, the surprise of discovering a dark green rhododendron in bloom — a reminder that the wind was not as cold or harsh as it seemed, and this was a natural harbinger of nearby springtime.

The second spring I found was in Montgomery, Ala., in late March. It burst upon me as the tropical isle of Tahiti must have exploded before Gauguin when he fled to paint an untouched world. I had been in Boston — still tightly buttoned-down beneath black limbs, brown earth, gray skies — and in the space of a few hours I stepped into a world vivid with camellias, azaleas, tulips, daffodils, and a dozen other shrubs and flowers. In the room where I was a guest a thoughtful hostess had arranged an assortment that brightened my room with such a variety of color that I longed to paint — or be a taxidermist of flowers.

Another definite spring had arrived when I was in Atlanta and in Washington in mid-April. Our region's urban capital, and our nation's capital, feature residential areas and parks that boast lavish blossoming for spring. From the famous cherry blooms that festoon part of Washington to the manicured lawns and dogwood lanes of Atlanta, this was a world made more liveable, more memorable in spring.

Last week in Chicago — there was springtime arriving all over again! Dogwoods and flowering peach and crab, Japanese magnolias, top-heavy tulips in hues to suit a Persian weaver's fancy — all these were at their peak. I felt as if I were a long-distance runner back at the starting line all over again. The calendar had turned back instead of forward!

Best of all, has been the spring I've caught in the mountains of home, however. The others were simply prelude to this good, better, best.

THE JOURNEY of our Astronauts to the moon is no

more remarkable, in many ways, than the journey our earlier pioneers undertook into the unexplored West of this U.S.A.

They knew as little about the terrain, about possible inhabitants already there who would very likely be hostile to newcomers, and they had no communications system by which they could stay in instant contact with those they left behind. If they heard from Eastern family or friends in a matter of months, rather than minutes, they were lucky.

Still the wagons rolled west, and although it is one of the oldest, most familiar episodes in our history, it remains one of the most stirring. Evidence of this came to us last week as we turned aside from a regular route and looked at two historic sties in Eastern Wyoming: The Oregon Trail Ruts, and Register Cliffs.

We climbed a small hill overlooking the North Platte River and there, indented in solid rock to a depth of perhaps two feet, were ruts which marked the passage followed by thousands of wheels. Exactly the width of a Conestoga wagon, they followed the hill, then showed where the descent began in what must have been a jolting ride. How many men and women, how many animals — mules, horses, oxen — laboring with all their might, had passed along this very spot. Comparison with our own situation made our automobile seem like Apollo 19 in its speed and gadgetry!

Nearby, at towering sandstone cliffs which rose above the meadows along the North Platte, was another unusual memento of the past. Register Cliff is testimony to man's universal desire to leave his mark on the landscape, to leave a message for others who may come after. Along the Oregon Trail there were three locations where travelers left their names: Independence Rock, Names Hill, and this Register Cliff. It is soft stone and therefore an easy tablet on which to carve names. Along the lower base of this immense, overhanging cliff, are hundreds and hundreds of names. Those of most interest are dated in the 1820s through the 1870s.

This cliff was popular because it was near the broad river bottoms which offered pleasant campsites and excellent pasture for the westward travelers. There was high mortality rate on these journeys (of some 55,000 emigrants during a peak year it is estimated that some 5000 died) and restful layovers at sites such as this along the North Platte were welcome. During the interval between hunting forays — while the women cooked and washed and tended to children — the men strolled up to the great cliff and left their names in the raw, lonely wilderness.

Their names are as varied as those in our telephone books today: Carson, Willard, Allison, Bequette, Carlile, Breed, Cordner. A few listed the state from which they had come: Illinois, North Carolina, Massachusetts, Ohio, Kentucky. One or two listed occupation; my favorite read: "The Oregon Wagon Train, Tex Serpa Wagon Master. 1859." (Without punctuation, of course.) Some were carved with the flourish of old school calligraphy. Others were uneven as a child's scribbling. And behind each name was a story — a search for something new and different, something Out West.

The sandstone cliffs are gradually crumbling. Wind and weather have erased some names with slow sure strokes. Nests, as of giant mud-daubers, scallop some of the overhangs. But with no other travelers nearby, in the still freshness of a Wyoming morning pungent with the smell of sagebrush, it is good to recall these earlier tourists who tried to leave permanent calling cards along the passage.

Montana: The fourth-ranking state in the Union in square

miles, larger than either Japan or Italy, yet with fewer than a million people in its borders.

The dimensions of that statistic begin to have an impact as soon as you enter the state. The great rolling plains to the east, the rugged fortresses of the Rocky Mountains in the west, the sprawling cattle ranches and the deep-gouged copper mines, the cities that are really only overgrown towns — all combine to verify the capsule descriptions. Land of shining mountains; big sky country; high, wide and handsome — and high, wide and lonesome.

Montana's capital city was built around a gulch. Three young prospectors from Georgia vowed that they would make their last effort at finding gold here in a narrow valley — and when they struck it rich Last Chance Gulch became the nucleus for the city of Helena.

There are those who contend that the real capital of the state is Butte, however, for that is the site of the Anaconda Copper Co., which owns all the copper mines in Butte and is the state's biggest employer and biggest taxpayer. The town calls itself "the richest hill on earth," a mile high and a mile deep. Many European cultures and nationalities seem to have met in Butte; its real melting-pot flavor makes it distinctive, while the immense open copper mine reaching into the city limits creates an equally unusual natural landscape.

It is not Billings, with its sugar and oil refineries, or Great Falls with hydroelectric power plants, mills and factories, or Missoula with the state university and lumber yards and paper manufacturers, that are the essence of Montana, however.

That is to be found in the towering grandeur of Glacier National Park, the lonely silence of the Little Bighorn Valley and its Custer Battlefield National Monument, the ranch-lands where more than two dozen kinds of wild grasses reseed themselves year after year and provide hay for great herds of cattle. It is in the forests of Douglas fir and Ponderosa pine and spruce, which seem endless until you meet truck after truck loaded with enormous fresh logs, and see the areas from which they have been cut. And it is in memories surrounding such places as the Big Hole Battlefield. On Aug. 9, 1877, a group of Nez Perce Indians, fleeing from Oregon to the safety of Canada, were attacked by U.S. soldiers. Of the 89 Indians killed, only 12 were warriors. The rest were women, children, and the elderly.

Carmel must be one of the most beautiful towns in America. Its natural setting is spectacular. On one side it nestles along the rugged, scenic coast of the Pacific Ocean. On the other side it runs into the bold, massive mountains which are part of the Santa Lucia range following the coast southward.

A white sand beach at the foot of Carmel is bordered by the rare Monterey cypresses. These trees are so eloquent in their contortions, whipped by wind and salt-spray and lashed by storm, that they are photogenic to the point of being make-believe. They express nature at her "arty" best.

Along the cliffs and on the promontories that border the ocean, homes of deceptive simplicity and elegance are perched. Numerous movies have been filmed here; film stars own homes; magnates of business and the professions have settled in this vicinity, along with those of less lavish means who have no less a taste for the grandeurs of nature.

Up the Carmel Valley and into the mountains are winding roads that lead to awesome groves of redwoods, sprawling ranches, and quiet hideaways of woods and grass and sunlit solitude.

In one of the coves in these mountains, Robert Louis Stevenson came many years ago, seeking health and inspiration. Until recently, the cabin where he lived was still there, nestled in its little cup of a meadow like so many weather-beaten, inviting cabins I have seen here in our own hills. The trees around it and the little spring are still there today. I like to think of the author of *Treasure Island* and *Kidnapped* and *A Child's Garden of Verses* enjoying the earth and sky and weather of this hidden place.

On the major promontory of land that thrusts out into the Pacific within the boundaries of Carmel there stands Tor House.

" . . . . My fingers had the art to make stone love stone . . ."

And the fingers, hands, muscles of Robinson Jeffers fitted together great sea-washed stones to build Tor House and its accompanying Hawk Tower on a treeless wind-swept headland above Carmel Bay. California's rugged and splendid northern coast, with massive mountains and deep valleys plunging down to the sea, provided precisely the natural background for another art possessed by Robinson Jeffers, that of making word love word. He constructed strong houses and strong poems.

A few weeks ago I re-visited Tor House and some of Jeffers' poems. The surroundings of each had changed considerably since my first visit during a long honeymoon journey.

On that previous occasion the poet, carrying driftwood up from the beach, invited two young strangers into his home for a long afternoon of conversation. Knowing of Jeffers' legendary coolness toward intruders on his time and privacy I was awed by his friendliness. Crouched low to the ground in recognition of the power of winter storms, the small house blended with sea and land in a kind of fierce harmony. Nearby Hawk Tower, which he had constructed of even more ponderous stones, with its narrow winding stair, seemed more a statement of defiance, of enduring nature's assaults. Here was the image of a poet and his work made visible.

Fortunately that image has been preserved. The Robinson Jeffers Tor House Foundation now welcomes visitors to the poet's home, hosts an annual festival and other events throughout the year to enlarge the audience for Jeffers's long narrative poems and shorter, more lyrical works. Unfortunately the reality of Carmel's valuable real estate and scenic beauty has made it impossible to maintain the isolation that was integral to this place in its beginning. The clusters of houses thickening on this promontory have almost buried the grey rock house and tower from sight. Loneliness becomes too costly a commodity here where nature has been so lavish with its gifts.

Rereading some of the poems I am reminded less of how the world changes. In his dramatic rendition of *Medea,* which became such a theatrical triumph, Jeffers spoke to us of characters and emotions which are as old as the ancient Greeks, as new as this morning's headlines. Tools, weapons, artifacts grow larger, sharper, more deadly, more life-giving, more useful, more trivial. But human hungers, tragedies, triumphs, remain.

Jeffers once wrote that when he first began to write most "modern" poetry seemed "thoroughly defeatist, as if poetry were in terror of prose, and desperately trying to save its soul from the victor by giving up its body. It was becoming slight and fantastic, abstract, unreal, eccentric; and was not even saving its soul, for these are generally anti-poetic qualities. It must reclaim substance and sense, and physical and psychological reality." He made a vow "not to tell lies in verse. Not to feign any emotion that I did not feel; not to pretend to believe in optimism or pessimism, or unreversible progress; not to say anything because it was popular, or generally accepted, or fashionable in intellectual circles, unless I myself believed it; and not to believe easily. These negatives limit the field; I am not recommending them but for my own occasions."

His occasions are often fierce in their passions, dark in their despair. But almost without exception they celebrate the stark beauty of nature and the will to endure. *Roan Stallion, Give Your Heart to the Hawks, Shine, Perishing Republic* : Their titles suggest their vigor.

I am glad that Tor House still stands above Carmel Bay, tended by people who cherish Robinson Jeffers' "art to make stone love stone," and fit word to word in abiding meaning.

SOMETIMES during these busy spring days, as I rush in and out on the back porch that is our handiest entrance from garage or lawn, I am arrested for a moment by a strange scent.

This is not one of the familiar smells which are part of this season or our region of the country. It is a "foreigner," it has been "brought on" from a distant place and another landscape and another style of life.

It is the smell of sagebrush.

Ever since I first made a trip West as a small child I think I have felt a strong affinity for the aromatic pungence of that plant which is, above all others, a symbol of the West that is myth and legend as much as it is reality. In the freshness following a welcome rain or under the bazing noontime sun, the sagebrush gives forth its essence in the distinctive spiciness which speaks of wide open spaces under a vast sky. Silence and loneliness. Scenery almost brutal in its beauty. The delicacy and savagery of the desert.

A few weeks ago we stopped in a lonely place among the Western hills and I picked a handful of the gray-blue twigs of sage. Their fragrance filled our car all the way back to the Tennessee mountains.

Real enjoyment was yet to come, however: On our back porch. Here, along a main thoroughfare of our daily household traffic, we have an unobtrusive reminder of a happy journey, other places, an experience too soon forgotten.

With so many events and demands crowding in upon us each day, it often seems that the possibility of savoring life has disappeared. Yet one of the chief delights of any trip is contemplation of its possibilities before it is undertaken and remembrrance of its surprises and delights after it is completed. If we cannot anticipate and recollect, we lose half of the richness of travel.

When I was a child my family usually took a trip each summer. I can remember pouring over the road maps weeks ahead of time, reading books and articles about the places we might visit, and discussing at meals and odd moments the adventure that lay ahead of us. On our return we had time to recall special days, places, people. And that is what my sagebrush does for me now! It reminds me of anticipation — and participation.

"WHO IS NOT a fool?" the great Horace asked in 25 B.C.

"The fool doth think he is wise, but the wise man knows himself to be a fool," Shakespeare said in *As You Like It*.

And Edgar Allan Poe once remarked, "I have great faith in fools — self-confidence my friends will call it."

How appropriate it is to have a day we can all celebrate as our own: April Fool's Day.

There are so many familiar bromides relating to the subject of fools that it is difficult to even catalog them. There is, of course, "fool's paradise," in which so many of our acquaintances dwell. "There is no fool like an old fool," and "a fool and his/her money are soon parted," as we would like to remind others who are not heeding our advice. As we all know, "fools rush in where angels fear to tread;" and as for those people out there ruining our country politically, didn't Mark Twain speak for all of us in "Huckleberry Finn" when he asked, "Hain't we got all the fools in town on our side? And ain't that a big enough majority in any town?"

Horace and Shakespeare and Poe make us all akin, reminding us in the words of another sage, "Every person is a damn fool for at least five minutes every day. Wisdom consists in not exceeding the limit."

Perhaps it is the universality of our foolishness that makes the fool one of the oldest characters in drama and fiction. Of course, in the days of monarchies the court fool or jester was an accepted part of the establishment. His intellect and insight might surpass that of the king (not a difficult achievement in many instances), his pranks and humor could relieve tensions and provide outlet for rancor in the court.

In his novel, *The Idiot,* the great Russian writer Dostoevsky provides us with the rich portrait of a man who is considered a fool by the world around him. "Everyone in this society is seeking his rights, and the common measure of these rights is money . . . into this society, where the fire

101

of conscience has become the reflection in everyone's eyes of burning rubles, the prince — like a knight with only his innocence as armor — comes." The prince, wealthy, sensitive, generous, is the idiot because "he refuses to be hurt or insulted."

As one critic has said, "The prince pays for the hurt that is visited on him by accepting it and suffering it, and by suffering it he breaks the vicious circle of hurting and being hurt, and by breaking the circle, he effects changes in others." Isn't this the central message our studies of battered wives and children, our knowledge of criminals, our social breakdown in many aspects, is telling us — that someone, somewhere along the route of experience must break "the vicious circle of hurting and being hurt?" And yet, how often today does our society label such effort as a fool's errand?

Compared with what we might do and be and become, we all share a common bond today. Happy Fool's Day, April 1 and the other 364 as well.

THERE IS a familiar saying especially appropriate for the restless ramblers of the world: He who would find the riches of the Indies must carry the riches of the Indies with him.

This time of year (and for that matter, any other of the four seasons of the year) my feet begin to itch, my eyes turn toward the travel sections of newspapers and magazines, and my imagination wanders along distant trails and among exotic scenes.

It is not that I am lacking in travel experiences. Research, speaking, and other quite valid reasons keep my suitcase in fairly constant use. Perhaps that is the trouble. I also want to stay at home. I suppose I have a personality that is split right down the center.

This morning the dogwoods in my yard are lavish with blossoms. The old-fashioned lilacs are heavy with the fragrance that is perhaps my favorite earthly aroma. Everywhere the grass seems a richer green than I can ever remember it being before. I have flung open doors and windows to the sweet warm air of spring and I would be content to stay here for months to come.

But . . . visitors from distant places arrive and their presence reminds me of places I have not seen, and wish to see.

A song, a sound, a smell, a postcard reminds me of places I have seen, and wish to see again. The quandary is as real as Hamlet's: "To go or not to go — that is the question."

But I have found one small solution to the problem. The variety of our region lends itself to reminders of many other places. I have discovered that right here there are scenes and moments akin to those that may be found in distant lands. For instance:

Driving through the mountains one day recently I looked up through the wisps of fog drifting along the highway and saw a dozen cattle grazing along a hillside. The grass was thick, luscious, tender. The cattle picking there were large, shaggy, reddish animals whose sturdiness seemed to match that of the steep surrounding slopes. It was a scene right out of Scotland. Even the mist lifting from the deep cover like a curtain revealing the emerald hillside and the patient cattle seemed born in the Scottish Highlands. Scotland in Tennessee!

The afternoon sun was like a spotlight on a field of mustard I glimpsed from the Interstate one day. That clear yellow glowing among the greening fields might have been lifted from a Van Gogh painting of the landscape around Arles in Southern France. The carefully tended acres there can take one's breath away with sudden glimpses of such vividness and light; and the same can happen here at unexpected moments. Southern France in Tennessee!

Along the highway from Tennessee to North Carolina after our recent rains there have been rivulets and waterfalls freshly born in every curve and cove. Looking at some of the long streams cascading down the steep mountainsides I remembered the splendor of the streams in the fjord country of Norway. Like glistening threads of silk they fall from steep heights hundreds of feet into the still waters of the fjords. Like loose manes and tails of rushing horses they plunge from percipitous cliffs and summits. Rushing, cold, these arteries of the living earth are akin wherever they may be seen in all their quickness. Norway in Tennessee!

On an evening not long ago I drove eastward toward the mountains with the western sun shedding its light at my back. And the shadows cast along the ridges and slopes below the mountains' pinnacles were the same shade of lavender and purple that I had seen bathe the hills surrounding the valley of the Ming tombs in China. This site is north of Peking, on the way to or from the Great Wall. Handsome structures rise above ground to designate the grandeur of the dead entombed below the priceless treasures. Leaving the valley late one October afternoon I looked back and beheld the rarest beauty of the day: The great barren hills throbbing with purple shadows that only nature could create. The same shades sometimes touch our mountains here. China in Tennessee!

Perhaps the old saying is true in reverse: She who would keep the riches of the world must look for riches at home as well.

AN INDUSTRIALIST showing me through his plant that had recently opened in our Appalachian region said, "Do you see that machine over there? It's the real heart of this factory. Its functions save time on every article we produce."

A friend of mine was showing me a new appliance that she had bought for a household that already seemed well supplied with every variety of gadget on the market. As a gesture of justification she remarked, "This is a real time-saver."

Daily we hear that some new thing or process or idea — if owned or followed or adopted by us — will save us time.

And at last we are prompted to ask, "Time for what?"

Here we are, surrounded by machines that are supposed to relieve us of much of the drudgery of existence, served by inventions that are reputed to free us of much of the tedium of daily chores — and we don't seem to have time to do most of the things we say we'd like to do.

"We don't ever seem to find the time to sit down and enjoy our patio (or porch or lawn or verandah or deck). I don't know where the summer goes."

"We never just spend an evening visiting with friends any more, the way we used to do. There doesn't seem to be time time for everything."

How often have you heard — or made — similar remarks during recent years? "I wish I had time to read a book or see a play now and then."

What's happened to all that time our time-saving devices

are saving for us?

Strange isn't it, back when our grandparents and great-grandparents had to look after a horse or a team of horses, and hitch it or them to a buggy or carriage, and creep along over an impossible road, they seemed to find more time to stop by a neighbor's house or hedgerow or yard than we do in our cars that whisk us to and fro with such efficiency. Odd, isn't it, that when those same deprived old-timers had no materials that would drip-dry and no machines that would wash-and-dry, no refrigerators to preserve and no electric stoves to prepare "instant meals," no cleaners that would abolish dirt with a minimum of muscle-power, they seemed to find more time to talk with each other, with the oldest and the youngest, than we do amidst the whirr of our household helpers.

It would seem that we're handling time a little like our Federal budget. We put a little savings in there and take a lot out there, and no matter how we try to disguise the reality — we're coming out with a loss. Perhaps our time-saving inventions are costing considerable time in their production, upkeep, financing, incessant improvement. Perhaps they are deceiving us into believing we are hoarding more time than we are. Whatever the answer, it's necessary to ask, "What's happening to all the time that we're supposed to be saving with all the gadgets we buy?" My balance sheet isn't coming out right, and I'm afraid I may be the culprit — embezzling minutes and hours I was supposed to deposit in trust for increase of a richer spirit.

WITHIN THE SPACE of a week both Elizabeth Taylor

and I were on the Harvard University campus. She was there first. Whether that indicates the principle of best-things-last or the theory of anti-climax, I'm not sure. I'm still pondering that question.

One thing is certain: Such juxtaposition fulfilled the doctrine of opposites: Yin and Yang, negative and positive, moon and sun, earth and heaven, the dual nature of life. In fact, contemplating the ventures and adventures of Elizabeth, I could find little but contrast with my own life.

Beauty. Well, we won't even go into a comparison on that score; violet eyes, luscious features, photogenic at any angle — from *National Velvet* to *Cleopatra* and in a thousand news photos that face became legendary. Meanwhile, some of the rest of us have had to mumble about skin-deep and inner glow and similar resources under our control.

Husbands. Between Elizabeth and me on this score it's strictly quantity versus quality. She has ranged over the matrimonial field like Genghis Khan raiding the camps of the civilized world; her conquests culminated in capturing the commandant of the American Revolution's Bicentennial, although civil war might seem to be more her forte. Having had only one husband disqualifies me from consideration in this chic, contemporary competition. But then if Elizabeth had ever had my husband, she might not have wanted any of the others.

Diamonds. Alas, the score here is also one-sided. Elizabeth's jewels have become as familiar to the public as New York City's deficit and erroneous weather forecasts. If diamonds are a girl's best friend, that girl is surrounded by close relatives. But some of my best friends are diamonds — real jewels, the kind you don't have to keep in a safety deposit box, enjoying the synthetic reproduction. And it taxes my imagination to visualize one of Elizabeth's egg-size baubles scintillating in the Harvard Faculty Club. There the sparkle seems to be of a less tangible, more verbal nature.

Success. With accumulated beauty, husbands and diamonds, plus a tumultuous reception at our nation's oldest university, what further certifications of success are possible? It would be acceptable to have a juicy role in a new first-rate movie, but as Elizabeth herself said with elegant subtlety, "With Robert Redford's and Paul Newman's pretty blue eyes on the screen, who needs broads?"

At this point I seemed to have discovered my only common bond with Elizabeth Taylor: I once wrote a book called "The French Broad." But even that bond fails me; the book was about a river.

It, and other books I had written, was the reason for my invitation to speak at Harvard, however. So perhaps Elizabeth and I did have some tenuous relationship. But the throngs that surrounded her — many of whom were reported to have protested, "But she's fat!" — were there to see a larger-than-life legend. The thoughtful few who attended me had no such expectations. Fat or thin was not the substance of our encounter. Yes, Harvard had Yin and Yang on its campus last week, even more clearly than usual. "To everything there is a season . . ."

WITH ALL THE old familiar tools of scales and balances, with the many new sophisticated methods of weights and measures, there are still depths of experience that remain unplumbed. These are part of what scientists as well as poets might call "the mystery of life."

Moments of encounter with these experiences do not

occur only in the research laboratory or the creator's studio, however. They abound in our daily lives, awaiting our recognition, demanding our response.

The mystery arrives under many guises. More than two weeks ago it presented itself at our front door wielding the heavy scourge of the destroyer. A few days later it fluttered the same way presenting a delicate aura of beauty. And if the first engagement provided an ordeal of surprise and loss, the latter left a memento of astonishment and pleasure.

When the tornado swept through Newport, touching down here and there as capriciously as an unguided camera focusing wildly from one point to another, we were out of town. We arrived home the next morning to discover our house and garage safe but our natural surroundings a shambles. A tall weeping willow at the entrance to our driveway, already unfolding its lacy mantilla of green in the early spring warmth, was uprooted. A great sentinel of a white pine, which sheltered the path to our vegetable garden, had crashed to the ground with such force that many ends of limbs were deep in the earth. And a long row of white pines along the western boundary of our yard was devastated. At least half a dozen were decapitated, their tall green crowns wrung off as if some giant hand were fulfilling the name "the twister." Limbs were strewn in mounds of disarray across the logs that had splintered beneath the winds, and pieces of the trees were driven into the ground as tightly as tent stakes slanted into firm deep hold beneath the turf. One large bough from the elm tree beside our house was wrenched from its trunk, leaving a fresh scar and an "empty place against the sky."

"Did you cry?" one man, knowing my fervent dedication to any living tree, asked.

I told him no because I was thankful no person and no part of our home were destroyed. What I did not say was that the sight was too awesome for tears.

109

We read of tidal waves and earthquakes and volcanic eruptions in other parts of the world, claiming thousands of lives, and such evidence of nature's power bewilders our feeble imaginations. One small, comparatively insignificant, example of nature's dominion can snatch us from apathy and smugness.

Several days after the storm our doorbell rang one morning. When I answered a little boy, wide-eyed with excitement, asked me, "Whose peacock is that on your lawn?" I thought I had misunderstood his question, but when I followed him outside I saw a stately peacock moving quietly across the grass, picking its way around those limbs that were still scattered in its way. Since I knew of no one in the neighborhood who owned peafowls, the appearance of this strange bird was all the more striking. Its iridescent blue neck and body, its proud comb, and its wide trailing tail, presenting a fan of gorgeous colors arrayed in an intricate pattern of perfection, introduced an exotic presence in our mundane, littered surroundings.

As we watched, the peacock daintily proceeded across the little slope, around the debris, and suddenly was out of sight. The boy who had first glimpsed it followed the bird briefly, then returned to his father's car in the street.

After the tornado, after the peacock, I went back to my typewriter and housework and daily commitments. The mystery of destruction enters our lives unexpectedly; we accept its challenges. The mystery of beauty enters our lives unannounced; we hoard its delight. We are glad that neither today nor tomorrow yields totally to measurement or forecast. Perhaps the essence of life's adventure is its mystery.

AFTER EVERY night's sleeping comes the morning and an awakening. After every winter's withdrawal and rest comes the spring and a renewal. After silence and despair the cycle of life and hope reasserts its power. This day we celebrate earth's awakening and human renewal and the certainties of dawn no less than darkness.

It seems most appropriate that Easter should be greeted at sunrise. No matter what corner of the world you are looking out upon, when you see it in the freshness and clarity of dawn it appears as you may never see it again. I remember several such sunrises so clearly that they might have been only this morning, rather than scattered through the years, and although grander, they imparted the sense of revival that is the essence of every Easter.

I remember a morning on Mt. LeConte after a brilliant display of the Aurora Borealis the night before. Clouds hung in the valleys below and lifted the pinnacle where we stood into some upper world of light and sun very close to the heavens themselves.

There was an Easter service in the Moravian cemetery at Winston-Salem, N.C., where, in traditional ceremonies, the Moravian band greeted sunrise with a burst of music among the flower-decked graves of the old burial ground of these early Carolina settlers. The music and the light seemed to merge into one golden moment, shining in sight and sound to pierce into the innermost self.

I shall never forget a dawn in Yosemite, when we saw the first pink shafts of light strike the great tops of the domes while the long waterfall still plunged in twilight down the mountainside, echoing across the dark valley floor to the ledge where we stood. Becoming part of the grandeur of nature at this moment refreshed all sense of human wonder.

I recall my first experience of morning on the desert, when one moment if was night and in the next breath, suddenly, it was day and the whole sweep of the horizon was bathed in brightness.

There was a moment in the old city of Siena, in Italy, when the streets were just beginning to come alive to human commerce, and the tile rooftops reflected a burnished glow that was mellow with time. The tapestry facade of ancient landmarks looked out on the sloping "circus" or racetrack in the town's square and caught the earliest streaks of sunlight washing the world with a beautiful bronze. Time seemed captured and illuminated in that moment.

Perhaps more than other early mornings, however, I remember those when I was a child and happened to wake up before anyone else. I liked to dress and tip-toe downstairs and open the front door and go out to look at the new day before anyone else had seen it or breathed it or used it.

If we could share an Easter gift this morning, I would ask for this rush of renewal, this awakening which is the daily resurrection of life.

Let us think of seeds for a moment. And a man I recently observed.

He was a "senior citizen" — but not too senior. His gray hair was crisp and thick. His tweed coat and flannel slacks were modish. He stood among the apple tree switches in the nursery, surveying them jauntily, eagerly.

I watched him as he read the labels on each specimen, then took hold of twigs and tested their strength, their resilience. He stepped back a few feet and surveyed the sapling from its balled, sack-encased root system to its uppermost spear. From one sapling to another he proceeded like a lively robin hopping across the April grass, pausing here and there to cock his head and make some invisible assessment.

He was so obviously a neophyte. The full-color photographs of glossy red and gold apples clustered on October limbs were almost visible in his gleaming eyes. Pictures of luscious fruit free for the plucking were obviously clear in his mind. Long winter hours of poring over the alluring seed catalogs and nursery brochures were about to come to fruition: The purchase, the planting, and then the harvesting!

Somewhere in that glad succession there is a gap . . .

Oh yes! Between the planting and the harvesting there is the tending . . .

Between April and August, September, October, there is the know-how and the sweat: the feeding and watering, the spraying and cultivating. There is the summer's toil.

Yet it is the seed store time of year again, and who can be bothered with considerations of freeze and blight and drought and insects and weeds and mold and disease?

There are the packets of seeds, enclosed in bright technicolor promises of what may come. There are the bins of bulbs, dry and brown and rough-skinned, waiting to burst into glorious bloom. There are the flats of tender, hothouse plants ready to try their roots in the rude soil of outdoor gardens.

And there are the shrubs and trees, scions of sturdy forbears who pledge future greening of the land (and probably should have been planted last fall). And all of these entice the garden-lover once again, whispering the old famil-

113

iar tokens of spring, wooing him and her to buy once more an excess of seeds, plants, shrubs — for it is spring and all things are possible!

I wasn't about to go up to my fellow tiller-of-the-soil in his plaid cap and his spring enthusiasm and advise him to remember all that would be necessary before his apple tree became a flourishing enterprise. Spring is for believing — and plunging — as autumn is for reaping — and resolving. Yet every visit to a seed store cancels out last autumn's failures. And I am glad.

I DROVE to New York recently and decided to fortify myself for the pressures and excitement of the Big Apple by renewing my spirit along the Blue Ridge Parkway en route.

The morning was glorious — not with sun but with fog. A bit frightening, yes; a slowdown in the miles-per-hour, yes; but providing curtains and backdrops for unfolding dramas of scenery, shifting of light and shadow. Clumps of brilliant azalea appeared in unexpected splashes among the dripping green trees along the highway. Acres of purple rhododendron became visible as the curtains of fog parted, then disappeared as the curtains closed again. And all along the way, especially as the fog burned away during the morning and sun and clouds were high above the mountains, the mountain laurel was heavy with blossom. (In fact, along one of the Interstates in New York there were miles of laurel blooming more profusely than I have ever seen anywhere. It made that thoroughfare seem like a parkway, leading through a gigantic garden.)

Rhododendron is more spectacular than laurel and usually gains keener attention from travelers and tourist brochures, but I suspect that many of us who live in the mountains harbor a secret preference for the rather quaint beauty of laurel.

Perhaps one reason for cherishing the laurel is its lavish generosity. How many times have we seen a mountainside denuded of every tree and sapling, butchered by ax and saw, rendered apparently hopeless of any future roots, and then found it in a few years time reclaimed by the gnarled green branches, the small glossy leaves, the clustered flowers of mountain laurel?

Old-timers of this region often call laurel "ivy," and then rhododendron is called "laurel." Strangers sometimes find this confusing. The term has even found its way into some of the geographical place-names in one of the old histories of the mountain region: "What are now known as the 'Ivory Slicks,' is a tunnel cut through the otherwise impenetrable ivy on the slope between the Hang Over and Dave Orr's cabins on Slick Rock, south of the Little Tennessee." The word "Ivory" obviously grew from "ivy," and it is interesting that the historian himself, who had previously referred to the bushes as "laurel," called them ivy in this paragraph.

Long before this man was writing, Bishop Spangenburg had recorded finding laurel near the present site of Grandfather Mountain, in western North Carolina, in 1752.

John Strother, who kept a diary of the survey between Virginia and North Carolina in 1799, mentions laurel repeatedly, both before and after crossing the ridge which divides the Nolichucky River from the French Broad. Doubtless many a surveyor for generations to come lost time and temper making his way through heavy growths of laurel.

The tiny blooms seen separately have always reminded me of polka-dotted Swiss material: Sheer, delicate white-

115

pricked by numerous little dark dots. Bunched together as they are, thick on every twig and stem, however, it is sometimes difficult to appreciate their delicacy. Perhaps its very abundance and beauty lulls us into taking laurel for granted.

I have not taken it for granted this spring — as its lavish bloom accompanied me on a long journey.

MOTHERS? They come in all sizes, styles, modes, descriptions. Yet one fact is inescapable. Each of us has one. Only one. Not a reasonable facsimile. Not transferrable. The human being of whom we were briefly a part, as close as heart and lungs and blood.

A day for mothers? Why not a week — or longer?

My mother? Contained in a single day?

Everyone should have such a mother. Then we wouldn't need those "tired-blood tonics" or such catch phrases as "generation gap" or silly symbols of "status."

My mother's lifelong idea of an afternoon of relaxation has been planting 13 azalea bushes or raking bushels of leaves from her wildflower trails. Her idea of an afternoon of hard work is attending a New York literary cocktail party as she once did with me. Her reaction? "A crowd of strangers saying things they don't mean to people about whom they don't care." Back to the wildflowers.

Which leads to the point that no one could ever accuse my mother of being a hypocrite. She has never hesitated so far as the memory of man runneth not to the contrary to state her age, claim her friends, or express her convictions. And she has not failed to hold convictions. My mother has not been a prisoner of her beliefs, however. She has known

116

that if they are healthy they can bear examination and if they are true they will be strengthened by reevaluation. While a sturdy faith has remained central to her continuing vitality, she has changed many routine convictions and scraped away many barnacles of cant and cliché. But fears of unpopularity or whims of fashion have never been sufficient prods to budge her an inch.

One of my fondest memories is a small battle she waged. For me it had large meaning. Members of a club to which she had belonged for many years discussed asking one of their number to resign. Her problems with alcohol had grown serious and become, to some of her friends (or should we say acquaintances?) "embarrassing." My mother waited for someone to defend this young, beautiful, sick member of their group. When no one spoke up my mother said simply, "Can you imagine what our rejection at this time would mean to this troubled woman who has been so generous to us? If you vote to expel her you take me off the membership roll, too." The discussion was closed. How many times in later years I have thought of my mother's simple little moment of courage and compassion.

My mother's idea of short-cut cooking is when you don't grind the coffee yourself. Her idea of food "worth the name" includes wild strawberry perserves (she loved it when I told her that "fraises des bois" were gourmet food in France), home baked bread, and a lemon or apple pie which is the despair of other cooks in the vicinity (including her daughter). Once she bought a frozen, ready-made TV dinner. It stayed in her freezer eight months. I never did find out what became of it.

It would be difficult to find anyone who loves her home more devotedly — or anticipates a trip more eagerly. And I never knew her to return from a trip without a little notebook full of names and addresses. New friends. The delight

117

of her return home after three days' or three months' absence is contagious. The pleasure of her presence at home, day in, day out, is infectious.

A Mother's DAY? Capture the sea in a teacup, the wind in a balloon, the mountain in an anthill. Mother's Week. Woman of unquenchable spirit.

I am nearing the end of my fourth week in Cambridge, Mass. The room in which I am writing is a pleasant study — desk, bookshelves, comfortable chair, air conditioning — provided to me by the Radcliffe Institute which has granted me rather special status as a Visiting Scholar. The room in which I have done most of my research is in Houghton Library of Harvard University. It is a spacious reading area, presided over by capable, watchful and helpful Keepers of the Flame. In this case, the flame being those treasured manuscripts which bring scholars from many places to discover their contents and interpret their meaning.

Each of these two rooms has a special significance to me. That significance embodies much of the experience I have had during these rich and stimulating weeks.

The reading room at Houghton Library, with its paneled walls, its leather-upholstered chairs, its bound volumes beckoning from the shelves, and its flow of boxes, files and folders across the desk — brought from hidden storerooms to the eager hands and eyes of some visiting scholar and reader: These are messages from the past. They are reflected in the title of a book written by Richard Kennedy about Thomas Wolfe, "The Window of Memory." These irreplaceable papers in the vast Harvard collection are windows of individual and

118

collective memory. Through them we may find fresh understanding of our past and awareness of our present.

The British author, Virginia Woolf, once wrote an important book, *A Room of One's Own*. In a very special and distinctive sense, this library enclave becomes a room of one's own to each person working there. The intensity and isolation of those sitting at nearby tables yet inhabiting, through their research, quite different worlds is astonishing – at once admirable and sometimes amusing.

The study at Radcliffe Institute is, in another way, a private refuge, too. A welcome, necessary refuge. Yet it has one asset without which I would have found it much less rewarding. From floor to ceiling, occupying an entire wall, there is an expanse of window.

From this window this morning I look down upon Cambridge's famous Brattle Street, where elegant old homes reflect part of the political and intellectual and artistic history of our country. There are also buildings of Radcliffe and Harvard in the scene. A white and pink dogwood are in full bloom, clusters of brilliant azaleas splash the green lawn in the distance with spring color. Leaves on the tall old trees are tender green, and warm May sunshine (which has been elusive enough in Boston recently) is flooding the day and all its components with golden light.

As I watch, students in a variety of costumes ranging from bluejeans and backpacks to navy blazers, from mini-shorts to maxi-skirts, are hurrying along the sidewalks. A tall, white-haired woman in sensible rubber-soled shoes carrying a folded umbrella tucked under one arm (a cautious New Englander, she!) is walking toward Harvard Square. A girl carrying a tote-bag loaded with books is pushing a baby-stroller and its tiny occupant along the opposite side of the street.

Every room of one's own also needs a spacious window

looking out upon the variety of the world nearby and afar. Perhaps that is part of the wisdom one searches to fulfill both in the mountains of Appalachia and universities everywhere.

AS I SIT writing these lines, a wind from the sea is blowing past me. A French window, reaching from floor to ceiling, is wide open. Beyond it a blue-black night has settled over the fine sandy beach, the fringes of grass which have found a toe-hold along a few small dunes, and the feathery sea-oats which grow in occasional tall, graceful clusters.

It is not the darkness, nor the scene it enfolds, which is the essence of my little world tonight, however. It is the sound of the ocean which dominates all else.

To a mountain person the ocean must always be a mystery, I think. The hills have their voices, too, and sometimes these are terrifying. But it is the constancy of the sea's sounds which impress a visitor from the uplands. The murmur and the roar alternate, the wave's crash is followed by the whisper as its water washes back across the sand and unto itself again. Crescendo and pianissimo recur in an endless symphony. It will be pure luxury to sleep surrounded by this sound tonight.

And yet . . .

That ceaseless movement and that irrevocable counterpoint it creates are part of the reason why I am never completely at home at the seaside. The sound is here — and gone, and followed by another seeming the same but never quite the same. The wave is here — and spent, and it is followed by another which appears identical but is not. The sand is here — and suddenly shifts under the assault of the breaking wave, and settles again, but not into the same arrangements, never in quite the same arrangements again. The breeze is here — and disappears, then rises again and carries its damp fragrance and its limpid sounds again, but each time new ones, fresh ones, never the same.

The trick of the ocean is that while it would seem to remain the same — the vastness of its reach and depth defying our imagination — in all its aspects, from the most awe-inspiring, it undergoes flux and irrevocable rearrangement.

Late in the afternoon we walked along the beach. Sandpipers explored the water's edge. Gulls dipped along the shallow places. And each wave which threw its net of water across the sand shifted the grains beneath or beside our feet. Tiny shells tumbled together and settled into new heaps of delicate color and design. Sand and ocean changed — again and again and again. It is the thunder of that change which rides the wind into my room tonight and brings me sensations I do not totally understand.

On a trip through Louisiana I discovered a most unusual place and story. At the town of Carvile, 75 miles north of New Orleans in one of the bends of the Mississippi, is located the only leprosarium in the United States. Located on the wide acres of an ante-bellum plantation, the imposing white mansion behind its moss-draped live oaks seems serene and comfortable. The human suffering and hope of which it is part provide a visitor with new perspective on disease and fear.

Perhaps no word in medicine conjures up more dreadful

images in our minds than "leprosy." For me, as for many others, memory of "Ben Hur," the book and later the movie, provided me with vivid impressions of the affliction that is also part of Biblical history. Victims of this illness have to combat not only their own physical pain but the isolation from their fellow humans that is born of alarm and misunderstanding. One step in overcoming the social stigma surrounding this disease has been re-naming it: Hansen's Disease, for the Norwegian doctor who described the microorganism that is its cause.

How did the unique U.S. Public Health Service Hospital at Carvile, for treatment of this disease, come into being? It was born of wretched misery.

"On a dark winter's evening in November 1894 a tugboat slipped away quietly from a New Orleans wharf. Hired to tow a coal barge up the Mississippi River, it moved under cover of night in a virtually secret operation.

On board the tug were the crew, a single doctor, and a small group of journalists. The gentlemen of the press could congratulate themselves on witnessing the completion of a successful campaign. For weeks their New Orleans newspapers had 'revealed the horrors' of a local pesthouse where a cluster of leprosy patients resided. Now they were making certain that these patients were deported from New Orleans.

Like most people of that time they thought the disease called leprosy was dangerously contagious. The familiar decree came howling down through the superstitious centuries: Perpetual banishment. Isolation from one's fellow man. So on that wintry night in New Orleans eight human beings suffering from Hansen's disease were herded onto a coal barge. (They were debarred by law from traveling on train, river boat, or any form of public transportation.)"

The night's furtive journey carried the six men and two women to Indian Camp Plantation: 337 acres of land, a ruined mansion, and seven decaying slave cabins. The largest of these cabins became the exiles' first home and hospital. Discouraged by the severe climate and the despair of his patients who knew there was then no cure for their disease, the doctor resigned after a year.

Then in the spring of 1869 four nuns came to Carvile. They bandaged the ulcers of these sufferers, provided hot packs for nerve pain, waited by the bedsides of those patients in reaction. They cleaned the old mansion of the cows and horses stabled there and of rats, bats and snakes. They brought comfort to the spirit as well. And they did all of this without pay. Within five years the sister in charge of the nursing died from overwork and repeated attacks of malarial fever.

But the sisters stayed. Other doctors became interested in the work at Carvile. Modern cottages replaced the slave cabins. The plantation house became the administration building for a U.S. Public Health Service facility. Today, an average of 135 patients a year are admitted and discharged. The hospital averages 350 patients at any one time. Resident quarters include cottages for married patients. Today's medication inactivates rather than cures the disease, as with tuberculosis.

Standing on the levee just across the road from this hospital and looking out over its giant live oaks, its manor house-administration center with long rows of modern buildings and smaller cottages ranged across the grassy fields, I felt that this was and is one of our frontiers. It is a frontier of research and rehabilitation in one of humanity's oldest afflictions. It is also a frontier of understanding and constant renewal of hope.

"THE FOG," Carl Sandburg once wrote, "comes in on little cat feet."

That was in his city of Chicago. In our mountains the fog comes in on giant padded elephant feet. Gray and silent it arrives, transforming the beckoning horizons of green pinnacles and ranges to veiled mysteries, indefinable, inaccessible.

Driving through the Smokies a few days ago I was reminded of how many travelers may always remember the region as wrapped in fog, since on a hasty journey along the thoroughfares this may be the only mood in which they will see our mountains. We tend to think of any place as perpetually appearing the way we have seen it, especially if we have visited only once and it has made a strong impression.

I remembered some of the places we had discovered in past years when the weather was not what is usually described as "nice." In fact, they were made dramatic and all the more memorable because of the moody, unsettled atmosphere surrounding them.

There was Mt. Washington, set like a towering forbidding crag in the midst of New Hampshire's scenic domain. For many years, until the discovery and measurement of Mt. Mitchell, in Western North Carolina, this was considered the highest peak in the Eastern U.S. Driving up part of its slope, then ascending by cog-rail to the summit above the timberline, where wind-gnarled trees and stunted shrubs give way to jagged rocks, we passed from a world of green openness to a dark, tormented landscape shrouded in fog. At the summit, where a strong shelter provided comfort after exploratory walks, we watched the clouds sweep over us, around us, permitting us occasional glimpses of the distant landscape but keeping us removed in a world of storm and stress. It was an awesome encounter.

At Mt. Rainier, in Washington, we had seen the snow-capped peak from miles away on common level ground, but as we began to climb the highway the summit became slowly veiled in mist. Then, as we came nearer and nearer to our destination, the mists began to part, reform, merge, move on. We rounded a curve — suddenly, like a giant curtain being lifted by some invisible hand, the fog rose, revealing a brilliant green slope dotted with dark clumps of evergreens and nimble, bright-eyed deer feeding in the tender grass. Beyond, rose the white crown of Rainier's mighty upthrust. It was an unforgettable revelation.

Then, on a morning along the Austria-Germany border, we went to Berchtesgaden. High above the luscious lowlands and surrounding lesser ranges, Hitler had built here his personal fortress called the Eagle's Nest. Following a tortuous climb by car and bus, the final ascent is made on the elevator built within the mountain for the evil dictator himself. We emerged into a world of darkling sunlight, but all the world below was covered with cloud. Aloof from the human world, one felt kin to Thor or Odin here. Then, unexpectedly, the clouds rolled away, and stretched far below were the tended fields and rolling pastures, the cherished woodlands and neat farms, the human villages. The vista was immense in scope. It seemed to embrace wild forest areas and small intimate homes where hearth and barn were the circumference of life's concerns. Stormy clouds surged in again. Once more we were isolated in another world. The Eagle's Nest of Berchtesgaden left an indelible impression in our memory — because the drama of the fog had yielded us the feeling a person may have when he feels he is separate from, above, the common, good green earth and his fellow-man.

And the Smokies — day before yesterday — alternately clear and cloudy, offering their scenes only in brief temperamental revelations . . . Perhaps it isn't "nice" weather — but it provides views and experiences heightened by the drama of

125

nature in full variety and wonder, no matter where or when we travel.

THERE ARE water people and land people. There are human beings who are part dolphin and whose feet must have a suggestion of webs between the toes. There are others who are part alpine goat and their hands seem to be especially built for grasping and holding and providing strength in a steep climb.

There are people who can spend hours gazing over an expanse of water. They find something new in each surge of the waves, every shift of the sand and tide. There are those people who can spend days looking out upon a vista of mountains and valleys. They discover some fresh shade of green or blue or smoky gray in the changing sunlight and shadow; the horizon is never the same to them — approaching or receding with different hours of the day and various seasons.

A friend who lives in Virginia's Tidewater country once said to me, "I could never stay in the mountains. I don't want to be away from the scent of salt air and honeysuckle."

And I remember another friend, a hiker and woodsman, who remarked, years later, "It's good just to breathe in these Appalachian hills, where the smell of leaf mulch and creeks and the deep forests with their ground cover all blend into some kind of heady draught, reassuring a person about the earth's fertility and the air's purity. I wouldn't want to live anywhere else."

A couple of weeks ago part of our family visited Cape Cod and Martha's Vineyard to renew acquaintance with this picturesque and historic corner of America. Work and play and every aspect of life is dominated by the fact that these are places oriented to the sea. Just as Jackson Hole, Wyo., locked in the towering splendor of the Teton Mountains, has a way of life which relates to rugged pinnacles and hidden valleys, so the coves and headlands and dunes of the Massachusetts shoreline and its islands shape a daily experience which relates to restless seas and unpredictable winds. Each — hills or ocean — offers its own message and rewards, each poses its own threat and hazards.

Between Martha's Vineyard and the mainland one afternoon the water became rough. Whitecaps rode the waves that appeared innocent enough, but there was a heavy swell underneath. We spied a sailboat in the distance, rising and plunging, tossed about in a way that seemed totally terrifying to a landlubber. But someone assured me that those who were handling that small craft were probably revelling in the challenge, the excitement. And I remembered flatland visitors who have come to our mountains from time to time — their dismay at some of our precipitous hillside roads and trails, their wonder at our impenetrable rhododendron and laurel thickets. We reassure them that these hazards are our challenge.

Sea water in our veins calls us back to enjoy and know the water. But essentially I am an earth person. Mountains rather than islands for me.

SOME PEOPLE collect rare jade. Others search for Indian arrowheads. There are those who gather stamps and others who hoard political campaign buttons and some who

127

assemble antique glass or quilts or butter molds. I share the enthusiasm of each of these collectors but only as a dabbler. My jade consists of a small specimen purchased long ago; my Indian arrowheads must be some of the discards those early artisans rejected for broken points or poor flint; my knowledge of stamps depends on an informed neighbor who shares frequent "finds" with me; I have a campaign badge, a glass cake plate, a colorful quilt and a butter mold that were in use when I was a child — and it is a bit unnerving to discover that they may now be antiques!

My true collecting lies elsewhere. I gather words, bits of speech, turns of phrase. My laboratory is without walls: It is anywhere I and other people happen to be passing or gathering. The various ways in which we use words reveal more than we might suspect: Our region, our race, our social affiliations and economic status, our personality, the immediate past that has shaped us and the future we shall be helping to shape.

In England I discovered that although we speak a language that is presumably the same, there are numerous variations. During a walk around Oxford a young friend said, "Now, we're going to putter home gently."

In the course of a day's outing through the Cotswolds the bus driver fascinated me with his running comments to arriving and departing passengers: "All right, love." "Come on, sweetie. Mind the high step there." and, "Sorry, lads. No more room."

At tea one afternoon I fell into conversation with a lady from Michigan. She had been to visit a meat market in Oxford and heard a customer ask for some "streaky meat." The request puzzled her. It pleased me. I told her that if it meant what it did in the Smoky Mountains where I came from it described bacon with some lean streaks in it — and it also suggested that the ties between Olde England and old

Appalachia were still present.

Few regions of the country have more fresh and distinctive folk language than that found in our own region. As Horace Kephart pointed out long ago, "Seldom is a 'hillbilly' (and he did not use that term disparagingly) at a loss for a word. Lacking other means of expression, there will come 'spang' from his mouth a coinage of his own. Instantly he will create (always from English roots, of course) new words by combination, or by turning nouns into verbs or otherwise interchanging the parts of speech. 'That bear'll meat me a month.' 'Granny kept faultin' us all day.' "

My collecting also includes succinct sentences, pithy statements that leave a lingering flavor for thought and enjoyment. One of these was given to me not long ago by a friend who has an exuberant way with words. Her memory is remarkable and with a few phrases she can bring an episode or a friend to hilarious or tragic life. Needless to say she is a delightful conversationalist. She told me that her mother's dictum had been: "Live graciously, think spaciously, and like things well done."

What might the world be like if we all collected that thought — and took it to heart?

Several recent items have brought to mind the old saying, "One person's superstition is another person's wisdom."

Or, as a French writer observed more than a century ago, "The superstition of science scoffs at the superstition of faith."

May 13 came on Friday this year. The day brought about considerable comment on national TV shows and a number

129

of private little knocks-on-wood across the country.

Examining a sample of graduation and birthday cards of the season I find that wishes for "good luck" are rampant.

Superstitions tell us a great deal about a tribe, a nation or an individual. In the Appalachians many superstitions center around trees and plants, birds and animals and the terrain. Perhaps the Indians who were here first imparted much of their sense of the mystery as well as the treasure of this natural world to the settlers who came later. And of course those settlers from Europe and Africa and the far corners of the world brought their own folk beliefs to blend and adapt to the Indians'. Owls. Snakes. Bats. Winter thunder. Black cats. Strange rock formations. These were the stuff of which superstition was made — and is still alive today.

Sometimes superstitions can have their funny side, too. Consider these remedies for a headache: (1) "To cure a headache, take a live frog and bind it to your head, and let it stay there till it dies." (2) "Eating the brain of a screech owl is the only dependable remedy for headache." (3) Catch a mole, allow it to die in your hands, and you can cure a headache." Comment: If I had a live frog on my head, a screech owl's brain in my stomach, and, or, a dead mole on my hands, I would certainly forget any headaches I might have had.

Then there is this folk advice for securing one's wishes: "Place an eyelash on the second finger and throw it three times over the left shoulder and if it disappears your wish will come true." Observation: A thrown eyelash is not exactly your easiest object to keep track of, even with bifocals. What if it disappears after that second toss — will the wish come only two-thirds true?

Two superstitions relating to children: "A child," I read, "should not be allowed to jump out of the window. It will stop its growth." I believe it. Perhaps permanently.

And, "If you sweep the feet of a child with a broom, it will make him or her walk early." And run, too, I suspect. As far away from home as possible.

"Never darn your own clothes; if you do, you will have bad luck." I personally can attest to the truth of that statement. And extend it to say that anyone else wearing clothes I have mended already has bad luck.

I learned recently that it is good luck to dream of a white house. Of course there are several very vocal persons in our country right now who are dreaming of a White House. Whether securing it will bring them good luck or bad, who knows?

We've sent people to walk on the moon and we can store zillions of facts on chips the size of a fingernail, untrimmed. But I suspect there are some of us who still listen to the owl's cry, hesitate to sleep with moonlight falling on our face, avoid broken mirrors and black cats on the highway and walkways under ladders.

We carry freight from the past that the computer may never measure. Wisdom or superstition?

A NUMBER OF efforts have been made during recent years to set some dollars-and-cents evaluations on the work done by housewives carrying out their routine daily work (if there is such a thing as a routine that can cover the wide range of demands, challenges, emergencies that make up the infinite variety of households in this or any other society).

Such evaluation cannot determine, of course, the worth of the most important achievement of any home; The creation of a human atmosphere where human beings can fulfill their highest potential or be encouraged and inspired to fulfill it elsewhere. Contributing to that, however, is a sense of the worth of everyone involved in this process. And since we live in a society where money — and the freedom and self-determination accompanying money — indicates our priorities and values, woman's contribution to creating a home should make her no less independent financially than her husband or her grown children. Without such independence she can arrive at old age, as we have seen many arrive, as a sort of charity case for family, friends, or welfare to sustain at their whim and conscience.

With this rather solemn introduction, I would like to mention one job that is seldom included in the list of the housewife's chores. Yet I suspect that many find it a part of their role. It is that of house detective.

Now I have seen the functions of cook, nurse, cleaner, mechanic, plumber, electrician, caterer, secretary, valet, answering service, entertainer, chauffeur, teacher, veterinarian, seamstress, playground supervisor (to name a few) listed as those expected of the more or less ordinary housewife — but I have never seen mention of her duties as a detective.

Granted that Sherlock Holmes or Perry Mason or Ellery Queen or Lord Peter Wimsey may have cases of more crucial importance, their clients may be more glamorous and their habitat more exotic, but the housewife-as-detective has the stimulation of the unexpected call for help, the sudden rally in the face of threatened crisis, no matter how familiar her clients or emergency may be.

There is, for instance, The Case of the Missing Sock (or Glove or Cufflink or Earring or any item that normally comes in pairs). In this situation, the culprit or criminal — depending on the circumstances — may be any member of the household, from the oldest to the youngest. But the search for said missing sock or glove, cufflink or earring, manages to disrupt dresser drawers, laundry baskets, closets, all those corners that are the special bane or pride of a housekeeper. By the time the mystery is solved (if ever), three other odd socks, two additional mismatched gloves, and another solo cufflink or earring no one remembers, have been added to the family miscellany. And someone is late somewhere: School, office, carpool, committee . . .

Or, The Case of the Lost Address. Someone jotted down — at a play or dinner or school meeting or ballgame or conference, somewhere — the name and address of a totally nondescript and forgettable character. But as soon as said character's address and telephone number are lost he/she becomes a Very Important Person. Identification must be located. Detective work on this involves reconstruction of the event, which pockets were present and therefore susceptible to search, which pigeonhole or filing box has space for another memo, and — if some time has elapsed before this forgettable person was remembered — just when the encounter occurred. Such situations provide openings for all manner of family discussion (sometimes called disagreement). "But you must remember . . ." It is fortunate if these cases are resolved without need of further, more professional detective service or the riot squad.

But you gather what I mean. Holmes and Mason and Queen and Wimsey always seemed to live in quite comfortable circumstances. I think that the housewife's role as family detective should also be included in her list of remunerative employment.

WE ARE IN the season of glorious weeds.

Botanists and farmers have their own specific definition of weeds, but for many of the rest of us there is little difference between a weed and a wildflower and a brilliant blossom to be welcomed and enjoyed.

Consider the royal colors of nature's pallette as the yellow of the goldenrod climbs its tall stalks in some of the poorest, most unlikely spots, and the lavender and purple asters, with their golden centers, beautify banks and roadsides. Their lavish blooms in the most common sites suggest that the colors of a king's court are late summer's gift to everyone who travels highway or byway in this generous season.

By the way, did you know that there is a goldenrod named for Roan Mountain, where it was presumably first discovered? Called "solidago roanensis" it is somewhat shorter, with less plume-like flowering branches than the common goldenrod. It is native to the southern Appalachians.

In some of the more shaded meadows and deeper coves, the Turk's-cap lilies are still nodding their tall regal blossoms to the passer-by. Their orange-pinkish-reddish petals, mottled with brown spots, suggest the kinship with those flowers we call tiger-lilies. The unusual curled shape of the Turk's-caps makes their name most appropriate, and the grace of their stems and leaves captures attention wherever they flourish.

Equally arresting when discovered along a mountain road or cultivated in some garden is the brilliant bee-balm, also known as Oswego tea. Its crown of showy flowers is a rich pure red atop a tall sturdy stem.

More ordinary — so common its very presence often remains unseen — is the wild carrot, Queen Anne's lace. Lacy it is, the flower composed of many small flowers brought together on a single stem, white and delicate as the most fragile needlework produced by a queen's lady-in-waiting. Yet its habitat, described by botanists as "fallow fields, waste places, and along roadsides," makes it as familiar as yeoman's muslin. Thus, with flowers as with people, is the proverb proved, and does "familiarity breed contempt"?

Let us hope not, for two of the most familiar blooms of autumn are also two of the most handsome. In marshes and meadows, along the margins of rivulets and streams, edging low wooded areas, the ironweed is now resplendent. Six feet and more in height, surrounded by the foliage of long slender green leaves, the ironweed brings a deep hue of purple to the late summer and early autumn landscape. It was the Frenchman, Michaux, early explorer and devotee of the Southern mountains, who first described and classified this plant whose color is appropriate to the French king and court under whose sponsorship he traveled.

One of my favorites of this season of glorious weeds is the Joe-Pye — or, as many people in our mountains say, the Queen-of-the-Meadow. Rich and subtle in its mauve and purple shadings, tall and graceful in its abundance, beautifying neglected places, it is forerunner of summer's passing and winter's arrival. Weed indeed! Queen of the Meadow.

WHICH DO YOU need most, a tantalizer or a tranquilizer?

Rushing through life doesn't necessarily mean that we're really involved in living. It can mean that we've found one way of avoiding real involvement. Like a motorist speeding along one of the Interstate highways, we're on our way (where?) so fast that we can't look at the trees, smell the fresh wind, notice the fellow travelers on either side of us. We need a tranquilizer to break the momentum of the speed we've built up. We need a tantalizer to break the crust of our suspicion of life.

Aren't we, in our cocoons of chrome and glass and stainless steel, a little too wary? "Negos" they're called in some of our schools — these who shun the risks of affirmation for the easier way of negation. "Negos" don't gamble on being "taken in" by a joke on someone, a belief in something. They wear the armor of pride and mistrust.

And I am reminded of Charles Dickens' description of Mr. Pickwick, the eternal greenhorn, the perennial victor in the game of living: "Pickwick goes through life with that God-like gullibility which is the key to all adventure. The greenhorn is the ultimate victor in everything: It is he that gets the most out of life . . . His soul will never starve for exploits or excitements who is wise enough to be made a fool of. He will make himself happy in the traps that have been laid for him; he will roll in their nets and sleep. All doors will fly open to him who has a mildness more defiant than mere courage. The whole is unerringly expressed in one fortunate phrase — he will always be 'taken in.' To be taken in everywhere is to see the inside of everything. It is the hospitality of circumstances. With torches and trumpets, like a guest, the greenhorn is taken in by Life. And the skeptic is cast out by it."

So many revelations in our public and private lives seem to foster our attitudes of suspicion. We do not need to be

136

totally naive if we seem unafraid of being open to life — with its wounds and its rewards; open to others — with their worrisome shortcomings and their wonderful talents.

Mr. Pickwick and all others who take in life and are taken in by it do not need a tantalizer or a tranquilizer. A toast then, to those who accept "the hospitality of circumstances," to the greenhorns everywhere who are "taken in" by Life! May we all be so fortunate.

WHEN I WAS a child my parents sometimes went to visit friends in the evening. These visits were totally spontaneous. They did not require prior invitations or appointments; they did not involve any committee meeting or competitive game. Perhaps the weather was particularly pleasant — balmy spring breeze lacing the air with the fragrance of honeysuckle, a cool dusk following a long summer afternoon, the sparkle of autumn or the brisk chill of winter. Or perhaps there was simply a call of human companionship — sharing family news, concern over some world event or issue, exchange of memories and a bit of humor.

Riding, or especially when we walked, I remember some of those evenings with a vividness prompted by no conscious effort. These were not remarkable occasions. The people were not international VIPs. Nothing which could be described as "important" took place during those hours. And yet, long after Red Letter days and weighty meetings and consequential holidays have faded from my recollection, these quiet moments come alive in my mind totally, richly.

When it was summer, the adults might sit on a wide verandah (it was a time before lanais became stylish) or on a spacious sloping lawn at another home (patios were just becoming part of the community landscape). The smell of dew-drenched grass saturated the evening air. Fireflies glowed intermittently across the lawn, seeming as large and luminous as the distant stars. The deep voices of the men, the lighter voices of the women, sometimes speaking solo, sometimes in counterpoint to each other, blended in a medley that became part of the night and the leisure and the warm, relaxed friendliness of an evening's companionship.

People still get together in the evenings. Each age group has its own area of activity. There is a foursome for bridge, a team to go bowling, a class to perfect our dancing or cooking or macrame or African violets. These are fine (I could stand decided improvement in each category). Sometimes we get together to watch television. (Even when we don't plan it that way it sometimes develops that we've come together to pursue the same program we watch at home.) And for the younger set there is a fully organized round of activity — at summer camp, at jobs and sports, and — yes, before the television. And these, too, are all right. Lives and days need direction. But is it necessary to have every moment filled? Is it always necessary that we be with our "peers,' participating in the accepted activities of our time and place? Is a quiet, unpremeditated visit to a friend, a leisurely conversaton, obsolete?

There is a great deal of talking going on in the world. The air waves are cluttered with it. Our corridors of power resound with it. If talk were all we needed, our personal and national dilemmas would promptly disappear.

But we need conversation, too. That's a two-way street. It involves listening as well as speaking. It involves ideas; the exchange of knowledge, the enlarging of understanding. Poet Henry Wadsworth Longfellow once said that "a single converstion across the table with a wise man is better than

10 years' study of books."

Conversation took place during those unremarkable, totally memorable evenings long ago. I wish that the atmosphere and the meaning of such an experience could be understood and revived today.

We describe someone as a good neighbor and it is meant to be a compliment. But is anyone's interest aroused by the term "good neighbor"? Does it suggest excitement or uniquiness or glamour or variety? Without good neighbors we would find it difficult to survive, yet we sometimes neglect, misunderstand and overlook them as we hurtle through our daily routines and crises.

Travel across Canada, from Nova Scotia to British Columbia, has provided some of my richest travel memories, ranging across a number of years and accompanying family numbering from two to five. Drawing from a grab-bag of recollections, I remember:

• The face-to-face confrontation with a grizzly bear on a path in Jasper Park. It was no contest; I abdicated and gave him all the room his deceptively clumsy gait required.

• Standing at Athabaska Glacier, a tongue of ice reaching almost to the highway from the great Columbia Ice Field, sensing in its chill blue color and creviced surface the presence of an ancient Ice Age.

• Reveling everywhere in British Columbia in the tall blue spears or delphinium, lavish and dazzling in their many shades from azure to purple; and in the colorful hanging baskets of the city of Victoria.

• The frontier excitement of the rodeo known as the

Calgary Stampede, with the snow-capped Rockies visible on a July day, in the midst of the rich province of Alberta.

• The red earth of peaceful Prince Albert Island, with sprawling potato fields, and the blue waters of inlets where fishermen follow the trials and rewards of lobstering.

• The Cabot Trail looping Cape Breton Island, revealing scenery of highlands and ocean, moor and beach, where the Gaelic language, tartans and bagpipes are reminders of the Scottish heritage.

• The green park on the Plains of Abraham, where flowers and lawn and monument commemorate the battle fought in 1759 between French and English forces contending for the supremacy of the American continent, where the leaders of both armies, Montcalm and Wolfe, fell.

These are only a few of the remembered places, experiences. Each is difficult to isolate because it is part of a larger fabric, a more intricate web of discovery and pleasure, surprise and satisfaction.

I wonder if the Gaspé Peninsula, jutting toward Newfoundland, still has the igloo-shaped ovens in yards along the scenic highway that links its lonely villages and farms? Freshly baked bread steaming from one of those ovens was delectable beyond description.

I wonder if the Chateau Frontenac, one of the world's famous hotels, still reigns like a medieval castle over the Lower Town of Quebec City, where history still hovers in the streets — and if breakfast overlooking the Chateau's Dufferin Terrace is still a delight.

I wonder if the country woman at a little crossroads near Crowsnest Pass is still hospitable to strangers who find themselves overtaken by evening shadows and chilling temperatures.

I wonder if the graceful statue of Evangeline still stands as a memorial to the 6000 Acadians sent from their homeland back to France or to Atlantic seaboard colonies, notably Louisiana — where their descendants became known as Cajuns?

I wonder if this "high, wide and handsome" land of immense forests, mineral treasures, fertile prairies, unique cities, two languages and unassuming vitality is as friendly as I remember it to be.

Perhaps I'll have an opportunity, or make an opportunity, to find out before long. Perhaps you will, too. If we must go somewhere — by plane or boat (and I once had a friend who built his own sailboat off the coast of North Carolina and sailed it to Canada), by bus or car, or even in imagination — why not go to Canada?

And say thank you for being a good neighbor.

THERE ARE TIMES when I like to sit and contemplate one of the paintings by old or contemporary masters recreating the scene of a summer picnic.

Almost always the women are dressed in diaphanous pastel gowns which float around them as lightly as thistledown. The grass is living velvet, the picnic cloth and the offering spread daintily across it are tempting in their perfection, and the sunshine shimmering from a translucent sky sheds only summer's gentle light and none of its sweltering heat.

There are other times when I like to read passages in poetry or prose which describe picnic outings.

Almost invariably the experience depicted is one of boundless pleasure and effortless satisfaction. Children gambol on spacious lawns or in well-groomed woods, adults spread festive arrays for an afternoon's feasting — or, in the case of twosomes, a jug of wine, a piece of cheese, and thou is supposed to provide sufficient nourishment.

Unfortunately, my experience with picnics contrasts wildly with those who have been exposed to such artistic varieties. Each summer I am lured anew by romantic visions conjured up when the word "picnic" is spoken. After weeks of juggling schedules and trying to pin down family that is as transient as a colony of summer grasshoppers, we decide on a picnic day and place. The venerable basket, with its twin handles that are growing only slightly tottery with time, reappears from atop a closet shelf and is rejuvenated by scrubbing and sunning. After minimal search, only a precious hour or so, the ice chest is disclosed in its hiding place. Paper plates and cups that have been cluttering crowded drawers all winter are assembled — only to discover that there are three short, and now there will be 22 out of the new package to clutter next winter's storage.

Food seldom requires more than a day or two for preparation. None of this loaf-of-bread-and-cheese for our family. Even sandwiches are considered only filler material. A picnic is a full-course meal — served outdoors, with special hazards. These include ants, bees, gnats, wasps, flies, chiggers, rain, wind, stray dogs, and other picnickers.

Out in the open spaces of woods or meadows, we all take seconds and thirds and declare, "Nothing like the good fresh air to give you an appetite." But since creating an appetite is not one of the primary problems in our family, we seem to be slightly superfluous in our solutions.

Finally, of course, there is the labor-saving aspect. I would judge that making a good picnic is not a bit more than twice the effort called for by a small state dinner. In fact, I always look forward to winter vacation when "getting everyone together" doesn't call for an "easy picnic" — just a three-course dinner with damask tablecloth and linen napkins to be ironed afterward. (I'd rather iron than scratch chiggers any day!)

That's why there are times when I like to sit and contemplate paintings or stories describing summer picnics. And why there are times when I just like to sit . . .

A leader in India identified seven evils which corrupt modern society:

Politics without principles
Wealth without work
Pleasure without conscience
Knowledge without character
Commerce without morality
Science without humanity
Worship without sacrifice

What tonic can cure us of any one of these plagues? What vision can make us whole?

When I discovered Paseo del Rio, or the River Walk, in San Antonio, I thought of the broad mountain river which flows through the heart of the town where I live. I thought of the wealth of folklore and history which are part of our region. Yet the streams, the rivers, the fascinating past, remain in many instances debits rather than assets in our cities' life.

Businessmen and political leaders and educational and cultural pilots in our communities have too little vision in dedicating themselves to the long-range development of our towns, our region. Worst of all, we — the citizens — do not give our energy and talent and continuing support to a demand for such vision and development.

So let me tell you about Paseo del Rio.

The San Antonio river was named by the Indians who first lived along its banks a word meaning "Drunken old man going home at night." The aptness of this name can be understood from the fact that the river makes a 15-mile horseshoe loop through six miles of downtown San Antonio. When the river was later renamed for Saint Anthony of Padua, its sparkling waters attracted those settlers who built a town, and it was used to irrigate the fields of the Spanish Missions. A Spanish saying was born: "Who drinks at San Antonio's river once, will drink of it again."

But gradually the river began to be a liability as well as an asset. Torrential rain brought floods to areas of the city built along the picturesque horseshoe turn. Then in 1921 the river broke over its banks and took a toll of 50 lives and millions of dollars in property damage. A flood control program was begun and flood gates cut the horseshoe bend off from the main stream during floods. There was serious talk of covering the stream with concrete and making a street above; the river bed would serve as a sewer!

In the mid-1930's a group of businessmen began to see the potential of the river area, however. A bond issue built an outdoor theater, quaint walkways and foot bridges. Then, in the early 1960's, Paseo del Rio was born. Its master plan was drawn by the American Institute of Architects, and it incorporated the style of early Spanish San Antonio with modern convenience and necessity.

Research into the past and awareness of the future has

144

created, in the heart of America's 13th largest city, a unique development. The river is kept at a constant level, and with its arched stone bridges it reminds many visitors of Venice in miniature. On either side of the winding banks are walkways bordered by trees, shrubs, flowers, and occasionally fountains and rock gardens. Along this way are excellent restaurants, interesting shops, a soaring hotel, and the theater where the audience sits on a slope on one side of the river and looks at the stage across the way. There are barges which provide taxi service for leisurely rides when walking along the river becomes tiring.

During the day Paseo del Rio is sunny and active and full of excitement. At night it is leisurely, with lights in the tall old cypresses and smaller trees lending a glow to outdoor cafes and the half-hidden entrances to shops and stairways and bridges.

What more meaningful example of local pride could other cities show than this: creating beauty out of ugliness, turning a liability into a treasure, incorporating a unique past into today's planning so that tomorrow won't be totally standardized. In the Southern Appalachians, where our once-pure, once-clear, once-abundant mountain water is a prime asset, it has become, too often, a hindrance, a drawback — a sewer for some city or industry. Old sites, properly preserved, can bring new money to a city, a county. Natural resources, planned for future use rather than present exploitation, can create prosperity. Most of all, imaginative leaders can change the face and spirit of a town or a country — if they want to.

145

Occasionally — not often, but occasionally — I am seized by the impluse to Clean Things Out. Desk drawers, dresser drawers. Closet shelves, kitchen hideaways: All those secret places where non-necessities gather, where, in fact, they collect with the relentlessness of small sea life amassing into great coral reefs in certain parts of the ocean.

Just before someone wrecks on one of our own special-blend reefs, I undertake to demolish the accretions of time and folly — and our squirrel-like tendencies.

No matter what the almanac warns or the zodiac says, no matter where the stars stand or supernatural forces ascend, however, my effort to Clean Things Out is doomed to ultimate failure. In fact, the inevitability of that failure has led me to formulate a law covering the whole untidy matter. I call it the Law of Instant Usefulness.

This law is based on the fact that the moment anything is thrown away it will promptly become useful. Disposing of any item will immediately assure its necessity and value. I can personally testify (volumes) to this fact. Witness:

I attack a basement cupboard of my mother's and heave out some old green glass bottles with attached stoppers which were once used for making homemade catsup (these came from New York state). A few months later I learn that these are the hottest items on the Early American antique market.

A piece of twine that has been an entanglement for every item in a catch-all back-porch drawer is dropped into the wastebasket. Within a matter of hours there is urgent and immediate need for a string just that length and strength.

In an assortment of caps, turbans, and other frayed and outgrown headgear that chokes a closet shelf, I select a particularly disreputable specimen of ravelled knitwear and dispose of it. A snowstorn the following week brings howls of dismay and grief (not to mention predictions of frostbite) at loss of this favorite garment.

146

A desk drawer yields up a collection of unidentified telephone numbers and addresses attached to names long since displaced in memory. These have hardly been whisked away before a letter (without any return address) arrives from one of the forgotten names with the reminder that in a distant city at some faraway moment we had promised to send our now-disgruntled friend one of our books. A reader (even for free) isn't to be lightly dismissed.

Yes, the Law of Instant Usefulness is still in force. Just try to throw away something you've saved — and see if you don't get caught by my Law.

"A FATHER is a banker provided by nature."

"Fathers should be neither seen nor heard. That is the only proper basis for family life."

These cynical witticisms summarize attitudes which we see shaping many private and public lives today. Yet one of the healthy changes occurring in our society is increased awareness of the father's participation in every aspect of family life. No longer is one parent excluded from enjoyment of the small moments that are more precious than jewels in the growth of a small human being. And no longer is the other parent excluded from knowledge of where and how financial security is maintained.

Perhaps this more total involvement in all aspects of fatherhood would underscore two other observations that we hope are more accurate than the two quoted above:

"One father is more than a hundred schoolmasters."

and

"What a father says to his children is not heard by the

147

world, but it will be heard by posterity."

How true — and what an awesome challenge.

In our own often violent world we hear the statistic over and over again: Fathers who neglect and brutalize their children were themselves abused children, and this is true almost without exception. "More than a hundred schoolmasters" taught those sons how to be cruel parents.

On the other hand, we daily encounter people who are upright, dedicated, garden-variety citizens unafraid to show compassion for others, unwilling to let greed for themselves and their own little families undermine that compassion. And it is not difficult to find the source of this commitment in an earlier generation, often in the influence of a father whose voice is being "heard by posterity."

The word "father" often brings to mind a word we shun wherever possible. That word is discipline. The first thought it brings to mind is punishment. But if there is any virtue a father can impart to his children, self-discipline must rank near the top. Consider all the personal and social woes that afflict us today largely through our lack of self-discipline: burdens of debt because we want more than we can afford, tragedies of divorce because we want our way and want it all the time, community neglect because we do not want to organize our time to include service to others, health hazards because we will not discipline our appetites. And these are only a few examples; we each have our areas of special neglect.

The man who might be considered in many ways the father of the modern world, Albert Einstein, certainly fulfilled the image of a father: Long white hair and white mustache, sad eyes, shy and friendly smile, furrowed face. Two of his personal statements on life's purpose might not be amiss on Father's Day: "Many times a day," this intellectual giant said, "I realize how much my own outer and inner life is built upon the labors of my fellowmen, both living and dead, and how earnestly I must exert myself in order to give in return as much as I have received."

He also said: "The ideals which have always shone before me and filled me with the joy of living are goodness, beauty and truth. To make a goal of comfort or happiness has never appealed to me; a system of ethics built on this basis would be sufficient only for a herd of cattle."

A father perceived by himself or his family as being "a banker provided by nature," can make a "goal of comfort or happiness" only. But the fall-out of deep happiness arrives with that self-discipline Einstein practiced and expressed in his effort "to give in return as much as I have received."

"One father is worth more than a hundred schoolmasters."

October, 1976. A trip to China with a group of Americans designated as National Leaders.

This China — covering more than three-and-a-half million square miles, about one-fourteenth of the world's land area, with more than 4000 years of recorded history — was poised at the threshold of change such as we could not have imagined during our brief but intensive visit.

This group of visitors included an internationally recognized authority on land use, a collector of Chinese bronzes who was also a major benefactor of the Metropolitan Museum, a World Bank representative, the Dean of Students of Princeton University, an archaeologist, a famous neurosurgeon, president of the National Organization of Women, a New York socialite, a Maryknoll nun, and a leader in family

149

planning, as well as a rising young politician from California and a distinguished member of the New York Bar. The variety of their expertise added a whole dimension of enrichment to the journey. (A different and no less fascinating enlightenment came from the manner in which each specialist shared his/her wealth of knowledge. But that is another story.)

As we crossed the bridge into the People's Republic of China, went through the routine of customs, quarantine, and changing dollars into yuan, and waited in the train station which displayed white lace curtains and crocheted antimacassars on the chairs, we reminded ourselves that the death of Mao Tse-Tung and the devastation of earthquake had recently shaken China. As soon as we boarded the train to Canton, however, and moved across the countryside we realized that it is hard to shake this land and people. Steep eroded hills, red soil, and evergreens alternated with the fresh, willow-green of rice paddies. Dark grey water buffalo plodded across the fields with a patience as measured as the passage of time. Huge baskets dangled from shoulder yokes borne by men and women burden-bearers. China is eighty per cent rural and the land does not impose an urban tempo on its dwellers. The rhythms of seasons and crops absorb political change, even nature's tremors — and continue.

Those weeks in China were unique. A daily schedule crowded from dawn until late evening took us from Canton (a big, busy city preparing for its annual International Trade Fair) to Kweilin (in one of the most scenic areas of China, where the seemingly endless mountains are like no others in the world unless it be the Meteora in Greece) to Changsha (center of important archeological discoveries and immense rice fields) to Wuhan (three cities at the confluence of the Yangtze and Han Rivers, an industrial center), to Peking (the capital), and to Shanghai, leading port and largest industrial

150

and commercial city. The distances were long and the varying landscapes invariably fascinating. Sensations of sight, sound, taste, smell, touch, threatened to overwhelm our capacities to absorb them. Ancient knowledge and new interpretations challenged our sense of history, expanded our world horizons.

Foreign visitors are not allowed to travel where and when they wish at random in China. Our schedule locked us in to certain places and times. Our lack of knowledge of the Chinese language locked us into a privacy most of us deplored. Within the cities we visited, however, we could walk, photograph, shop as we wished, except — and this was a large exception — for photographing the great political wall posters in Shanghai. These posters, called "dazibao," are actually a blend of cartoons and manifestos plastered on walls, fences, billboards, public buildings, to inform the public about political enemies or leaders. Crowds, often numbering in the hundreds, gathered around these posters as they caricatured Madam Mao and her cohorts and denounced those who might have supported them. We were forbidden to take pictures of any of these posters; no satisfactory reason for this denial was ever provided.

There are more than 5000 rivers in China. The largest, of course, are the Yangtze and the Yellow. I must admit that as I crossed the Yangtze and watched its mighty swirling waters, I remembered the romance of childhood geography lessons, the tragedy in news stories that used to tell of devastating floods along the Yangtze's serpentine course. And I was interested that the international economist in our group told me that he found China's harnessing of its waterways, its abolition of destructive floods, one of the most interesting aspects of our trip.

151

Tea-and-briefing.

This is the ritual — one part social, one part educational, one part political — to which visitors in China must become accustomed.

The social reason for tea-and-briefing expresses the natural hospitality of the Chinese people. Everywhere we went we found a long table, usually covered with a paper or oil cloth in brightly colored decorations, and a covered tea mug at each place. Scattered down the length of the table were cigarettes and ash trays, matches in pretty little boxes, and occasionally saucers of peanuts or some other specialty of the region.

The fact that only one person in our group smoked was a source of considerable and constant astonishment to our Chinese hosts. Many of them smoked with an enthusiasm that would gladden the heart of any tobacco manufacterer.

The tea was the green Chinese tea with leaves in the cup; no cream, lemon or sugar. Constantly replenished, often from a metal tea kettle, it was kept at a temperature slightly above scalding. I went across China with a blistered tongue.

Have you ever been to tea at a bridge? Have you ever been to tea in a subway? There seems to be no place in China where it is impossible to have tea-and-briefing. At schools and museums, hospitals and industrial exhibits, theaters and crafts centers, factories and farms, train stations or amusement parks, we found tea-and-briefing. And in the big administration room on a bank under the great Yangtze bridge at Wuhan we sipped tea and received a briefing on the building and meaning of the bridge while trains and buses and trucks thundered by overhead.

In a long, immaculate, marble passage leading to the Peking subway we discovered a table laid for tea-and-briefing. The New Yorkers who were with us tried to picture such an event in the BMT in their city; it was an effort of the imagination that proved totally unsuccessful.

The educational aspect of these occasions helped us gather the vital statistics and history of whatever, wherever, we were visiting. Thus our informants exposed us to knowledge that could help us understand what we were seeing in fuller context. The cost and achievements of the Yangtze bridge or Peking subway, the courses of study and school enrollments, medical treatments at clinics and hospitals, production at factories, crops in agricultural communes; such information filled our notebooks as we gulped tea, listened, and asked questions, sometimes naive, sometimes penetrating.

Political instruction permeated each tea-and-briefing. Evils of the Old Society were catalogued fervently and repeatedly. Even more objective history has recorded many of those evils and failures, reflecting inhuman oppression and cruelty.

But the complusion to make the present seem perfect leads to skepticism rather than conviction. "Soldiers, workers and peasants" are given credit — as emperors and scholars once were — for all wisdom and goodness. So far in human history, however, it remains to be proved that any group of people merits unrestricted authority over any other group of people, or possesses total virtue. Thus, political doctrine was less successful than the social and educational functions of tea-and-briefing.

For quite a while after arriving home I could not sip a cup of hot tea without waiting for a lengthy briefing, in Chinese translated through an interpreter, to begin. "We warmly welcome American friends . . ." And their tea confirmed that they meant warm.

153

I mention some everyday incidents, the sort of things guidebooks often overlook and more learned travelers dismiss in favor of weightier matters. Sometimes they can bring a place alive, etch it in memory more decisively than the Very Important Events that are planned and purposeful.

First, there was the countryside — varying from Canton in the south to Peking in the north, more than a thousand miles as we traveled, as much as our deep South might vary from the Midwest or parts of New England to the north. And yet, whether the crops were rice or wheat, cotton or corn, whether the animals were the great grey water buffalo or stout little Mongolian horses and mules as well, whether the headgear of the workers was the wide straw hat that makes every green paddy look like a picturebook illustration or a fur-lined cap with plump ear flaps dangling from each side — no matter what the landscape, it seemed to be throbbing with activity. Men and women carrying water or distributing it over the fields with dipper-like motions from the canals threading the cultivated plots; men and women planting, cultivating, or harvesting in a wide field that stretched to the horizon; men and women carrying loads of bricks or other materials to build a dwelling or barn or storehouse; men and women constructing new roads or buildings in countryside or village; these and dozens of other chores, accomplished in so many instances chiefly by human labor rather than the machine, appeared to be part of a ceaseless cycle of daily and seasonal work.

Along the roads and highways this same ebb and flow

went on. It cannot be described as hustle or bustle because that was not the tempo, not the feeling. Perhaps the motion could best be understood as a pulse. Along certain highways, in certain areas, it beat at a faster tempo, sometimes — as in the late afternoon and early evening when the day's labor was winding down — it slowed to a more plodding gait. Farmers let their buffalo graze along stream banks or on the grass beside the roadway. People paused for a few moments of conversation with one another. But the undercurrent flowed on: A landscape in motion.

Another impression that strikes the visitor with force is that of crowds — specifically the crowds he or she attracts whenever venturing out alone or with only one or two other Americans. To walk down the street accompanied by a group of 40, 50, 60 people, all examining your dress, countenance, actions with complete and undisguised curiosity, is an exercise in self-consciousness. To go into a big department store for some "window" shopping, or — if luck is with you — for some actual purchases, and find yourself surrounded by an aisle overflowing with an audience watching, nodding, smiling, watching, frowning, watching, is another exercise in loss of composure. At least, there is never any fear of loneliness when walking the city streets of China.

People — and place — these two inextricably related, powerful, the essence of China experience.

The health of almost a billion people (at the time of our visit in 1976, now it is a billion) presents an awesome challenge. Life traditionally has been held cheap in this most ancient of continuing civilizations. As we drove along the

Pearl River in Canton, our introduction to China, our guide said that at least ten thousand people used to live on sampans on the river. The senior statesman in our group, who had visited here in 1921, assured us that a more accurate estimate would be one hundred thousand sampan dwellers. When he ventured on the streets each morning it was not unusual to see bodies of those who had died of hunger or disease during the night. River people were forbidden to marry land people. Sampan people bore the brunt of a deadly discrimination.

This was only a small example of the past suffering and waste of centuries. Smog blanketing many of the cities, dust sifting across great patches of the countryside, and the constant sound of coughing and spitting suggested current health problems.

Our visits to hospitals and clinics introduced us to the "barefoot doctors," those, we were told, "who are involved in practical life and rural areas." They are paramedics who go out into villages and homes; their work is highly praised.

We were also introduced to the use of acupuncture in surgery. In Canton the forty-one year old woman smiled at us as stainless steel needles ("in the old days they were silver") were placed in legs, arms, and the palms of her hands. We watched the surgery for a tumor of the thyroid. And as the sheet covering her legs fell slightly askew at one point, we noticed the thick callouses on her feet. How many miles had she walked along those paths between her dwelling and her work in the fields; how many miles had she trudged in nearby rice paddies?

Witnessing removal of a brain tumor at the hospital in Wuhan was a riveting experience, especially with our own neurosurgeon to advise us what was happening at each step. (And although much of the equipment was out-moded by our standards, he judged the techniques and surgical skills

156

to be excellent.) The scalp was peeled back, blood vessels were cauterized, and use of a surgical hand auger and saw loosened a piece of skull like a tortoise shell. This was lifted away. Carefully, slowly, carefully, slowly, down into the brain the surgeon inched. At last the tumor was teased out of its dark resting place. Huge, ugly, it lay in the surgeon's hand and seemed as large as a child's fist. Carefully, slowly, began the reverse procedure of closing all the delicate webs of life which had been opened. How fragile and how tough is the human body. What a miracle of design weaves blood and bone, muscle and skin, water and minerals and every ingredient in the physical whole into a creature akin to all others of the species and yet invariably unique.

A phrase we heard many times asserted the combination of traditional Chinese and Western medicine. Western medicine is that which makes use of technology and recent pharmaceutical developments; traditional medicine relies on acupuncture and herbal as well as other cures. In several clinics and hospitals we were shown some of the herbs — and I discovered a link with the Southern Appalachian Mountains.

On a shelf of the traditional remedies I spied ginseng. Our Chinese guides and even my fellow Americans were surprised to learn that this valuable root was "native" to Southern Appalachia. Among mountain people it is sometimes called "sang" and it has a long and international history.

In 1794 André Michaux, a French botanist, journeyed through the Southern mountains, found ginseng in the rich shaded coves, told the hill people about its value in the Far East, and showed them how to dig and prepare it for shipment.

In 1849, New York reporter Charles Lanman, traveling down the French Broad River from Asheville, North Carolina, to Paint Rock, Tennessee, met a man who appeared to be an illiterate mountain farmer with little awareness of the outside world. Lanman was astonished when the native questioned him about recent news from China. Further conversation revealed that the old fellow was a "sang digger" and the roots he collected were shipped to China and Korea.

Ginseng is the oldest export of South Korea's capital, Seoul. And there is a modern "ginseng festival" in Hong Kong, aimed at stimulating sales of the cultivated plants. But it is the wild ginseng which has always been most highly prized. The older the plant the larger and more pronounced are the twin prongs which lend the root resemblance to the human body. Its Indian name in Iroquois is "garentouges," meaning "human thigh." Ginseng derives from the word "jen-shen" in the Peking dialect, "man-like." The root's value comes from the Chinese doctrines of signatures which suggests that any medicine brewed from a plnat having the same shape as the afflicted limb or organ will be effective. Since many ginseng roots resemble the complete human figure, it has been considered a remedy for many ills.

According to Western medical annals there is no known human condition it has cured. Useless? Perhaps, but far from worthless. Its market value has often been twice its weight in gold. And who would dispute with the doctors and nurses across China who have it on their shelves today as part of their traditional medicine?

Back in the days of Virginia's famous Colonel William Byrd of Westover he was writing that he had chewed a ginseng root "which grows in the mountains of Tartary and at the Cape of Good Hope and in the Appalachian mountains of America, but as sparingly as truth and public spirit." The inconspicuous green stem with three large and two small leaves is now one of the rarest plants in America. (As rare as truth and public spirit?)

Ginseng forms a bond between two regions of the world which are far apart in history and politics but share a common hope for finding the elixir of life, either in a rare wild root or in its trade.

SHE WAS a small woman — her hand reaching only to my shoulder — and lean, too, unlike many of the older Chinese women who are plump. Only her face and hands and bare feet were visible from under her severely pulledback black hair and the loose black trousers and blouse whe wore. These features revealed the nature of her life, however: Hard work indoors and in the rice fields, adapting to changes in the natural world and in the affairs of state as they reached down from distant centers of power to her small home.

A half-dozen of us were visitors in her home one bright October morning. Our official hostess was a daughter-in-law, 27 years old, who spoke English and could describe for us the daily life about which we were so curious. But it was this older one, who did not speak English but who looked at each of her visitors with such birdlike brightness, who communicated the spirit of the household. She reminded me of strong, modest Appalachian mountain women or women on our Western plains, ready to be friendly but not assertive, eager to know and yet not intrude. Her smile creased her face into dozens of furrows like dry earth cracking under sudden sunlight.

The commune where this family lived was outside the city of Kwangshow (Canton) in Southeast China. The size of communes varies throughout China, but they are roughly the size of an English county and usually contain a country town and several villages. Each village makes up a production brigade and the brigade consists of production teams. Thus, through the production team, which works as a unit and manages the labor and income of its members, following quotas which are set at a higher level, the individual relates to brigade and the brigade to the commune and the commune to the overall government.

There were 69,000 people in the commune we visited, with 25 production brigades and 299 production teams. They grew two crops of rice a year, winter wheat, peanuts, sugar cane, livestock and fish; their factories repaired farm machinery and produced bicycle parts, umbrellas and bricks. There were 25 primary schools and three "middle" schools for some 13,000 students. A clinic offered both Western and traditional medicine.

At the heart of all this organization and all the statistics, however, were the people, their daily lives. In one long complex of dwellings, we entered one home. Dim, neat, sparsely furnished yet seeming crowded, it expressed the life of both an old and a new China. The wooden rafters overhead supported a peaked tile roof; the floor was of square red clay bricks. Near the ceiling, out of reach from the floor below, was a wide shelf full of handwoven old baskets and crocks for storage; in one corner of the room were wooden measures and homemade tools; elsewhere well-used straw brooms leaned against the wall. These things, too, reminded me of similar baskets, tools, brooms made in my mountains for daily use.

In the middle of the room sat a short round table. A single light bulb dangled from the ceiling. A clock and numerous brightly colored pictures and the ubiquitous countenance of Chairman Mao decorated the walls. A small radio and three flashlights were on top of a chest of drawers. Several wooden chairs and stools accommodated the visitors. And the shini-

160

est, apparently the most prized possession in the house — even more esteemed than the two bicycles — was the sewing machine. We were to notice many times throughout the journey across China, in stores and homes, the pride in owning a sewing machine.

Besides this central room the home contained two bedrooms and a small kitchen. Living here were a young married couple, the man's mother, their two children aged 5 and 1 years, and three of the husband's younger brothers. All except the mother-in-law and the baby had work or school away from home. Any leisure was spent in studying the thoughts of Chairman Mao and evaluating the success with which various family or neighbors were fulfilling those instructions. Here, flashes of similarity between my place and this place were as distant as the miles around the globe which separate them.

As we left, I asked the mother-in-law if I might take her picture. She seemed both pleased and abashed. Others must have their pictures made with her. Outside, in the square little courtyard with its water trough and line of towels and wash cloths, my lens focused on her weathered, enduring, lively countenance. And she looked straight at the camera and smiled at the stranger behind it.

HISTORIES, CRITIQUES, memoirs and statistics dealing with the art and politics of China are available in abundant quantities. It surprises me that there are so few volumes which include effective description or even appreciation of the landscape of that vast and varied country.

Just as no visitor to America can have full understanding

of our national character and devotion to our land if he/she has seen only New York, Chicago, Atlanta and Los Angeles — missing the expanses of our great prairies, the majesty of the Grand Canyon, the rocky shores of New England, or our own green Appalachian Mountains — so, too, a traveler in mainland China needs to relate to the natural world in all its wonder. This is necessary not only because the scenery itself is so extraordinary but also because so many of the people (some 80 per cent of the population) live in rural areas.

Rivers and hills, fields and paddies, sun and rain and wind define their lives. Horns of buses and military trucks along new highways may signal an acceleration of the pace of life in the cities, but the rhythms of the countryside are those of the bicycles which are everywhere and those of the water buffalo in the south and the tough little Mongolian horses or shaggy donkeys in the north, beasts of burden and of cultivation for the rice, wheat, millet and food crops to feed a billion people.

Seen from the air, from a train or through the windows of a bus, the patterns of the rice fields offer such a perfect artistry that they seem to have been designed by some master craftsman. From a distance there is no reminder that this willow - green brilliance and heavy yield has been nourished by night-soil (human fertilizer which has been treated and brought from the villages and cities — nothing is wasted in China). As patchwork after patchwork of fields in various stages of planting, cultivation and harvest unfolds during even the briefest trip, the amateur photographer is frustrated: There is no way to capture the broad expansive beauty of these scenes and share them with others. A suggestion, a glimpse only is possible.

And how much more challenging to try to seize the splendor of the mountains of Kweilin. I knew nothing of this city or region when I was told we would visit there. I didn't

162

even know how to pronounce its name (Kway-lean) or where to look for it on the map (northwest of the city of Canton). Then I learned that for centuries Chinese artists had gone to this place for inspiration. Much of the scenery depicted in Chinese paintings reflects the influence of the landscape around Kweilin. In recent years few foreign visitors had been permitted to include this area on their itinerary; what a loss it would have been in my mind and memory to have been deprived of this experience.

Approaching Kweilin from the air, a traveler feels that the ancient countenance of this earth is gathered into its deepest wrinkles here. Barren domes and pinnacles, these mountains rise abruptly from valley floors, tall, pointed, misshapen as witches' Halloween hats. These limestone masses are not few in number or confined to a small scenic area: They cover an area of some 230 square miles — horizon fading into horizon as the viewer seeks to grasp and encompass this monumental evidence of the earth's erosion.

During the stay in Kweilin our group was taken on an all-day trip down the Li Kiang. This river winds through remote countryside, providing glimpses of the daily life of farmers and boatmen along its course. It also cuts through narrow gorges and green plains surrounded by the towering peaks which shade from grey to blue to green to dusky lavender according to the slant of the sun, its lights and shadows. People and nature combined to make this day a feast of the senses.

Much of the life of the villages along the river's course was centered along its banks: Cultivating small patches of ground, cutting bamboo, washing, carrying water in buckets swinging from a shoulder yoke, towing a boat upstream by means of long ropes tied around men's and women's waists. There was also much life on the river: Junks with their colorful sails like paper playthings, some with families

163

living aboard — elderly grandparents and small children along with the working adults. The cormorant fishermen were there, too: Men with long shallow boats and large baskets into which they gathered the fish their trained cormorants brought to them after dives into the water.

Beside us, before us, behind us, all the day: The majestic upthrust mountains. The golden October light of late afternoon on the Li Kiang melted these monarchs into a dreamlike lost horizon. Having returned, having left it so far behind, a sojourner wonders if that landscape was all imagined — and shares consolation with those generations of artists who have tried to translate onto paper or canvas the magic of Kweilin's scenery.

THE WIND.

At the Great Wall of China the presence that greets you, seizes you — shaking and addling you somewhat as a mastiff may shake a terrier in its grip — is the wind.

This is not a wandering shift of breezes, not a sudden gale rising and subsiding in unexpected storm. This is a natural force which unites with the man-made wonder you have come to see, creating another dimension of the bold, stark scenery. The Wall challenges. The wind assaults. Mind and body are stripped of niceties before the harshness of this Wall and wind. Survival is all.

Wind at the Great Wall is the enemy: Keen as a knife-blade, brutal as an ax, penetrating as an arrow. Its presence would have given the ancient toilers along jagged mountain crests a daily antagonist against which to pit their muscles' strength and their minds' sanity. Assuaging their emperor's

164

fear, erecting a barrier against predatory strangers from the north, the rude, slaving laborers could feed their resolve and renew their exertions by the heat of their dull, constant anger against the lashing of the wind. Their deadened minds honed under the sawing whetstone of wind, their calloused bodies punished each day anew by wind, they could fight it, deny it, defy it by constructing slowly, laboriously against it: This Wall.

The traveler comes to the Wall gradually and with effort. As the level plain around Peking is left behind, as the busy thoroughfares leading in and out of the capital dwindle into country roads, the bus's motor churns and growls beginning its climb into the hills. The smooth surface of a modern highway gives way to the rocky roadbed of a passage hewed out of the mountainside. Small stone farmhouses blend into the stony landscape, their grey chill softened by garden patches and occasional persimmon trees splashing round orange fruit against the October sky. On and up the bus toils, tossing its passengers against each other as carelessly as a buffing machine tumbles rough stones together to polish them.

A train appears in one of the narrowing valleys, following the rail line from Peking to a station below the Great Wall. In the shadow of the looming mountains these man-made vehicles — train, bus, the heavy trucks along the pitted, rutted road — appear almost as toys.

The heights grow more precipitous, vegetation has dwindled to low tough grasses and shrubs. Everywhere are steep barren ridges. Then, suddenly, outlined along the highest, farthermost pinnacle: The Wall.

Other views break into sight. Like a monstrous serpent the Wall undulates along the contours of the mountaintops, dipping and rising, deceptively graceful in its might. The bus parks; riders disembark and hurry toward the stone steps

165

leading up onto the roadway atop the Wall. On either hand it stretches away from you, even its length an ambiguous number in your mind. 1400 miles, counting as the crow flies. Considering loops and doubling back and contours, probably twice 1400. Or, the distance from New York to Los Angeles, one authority says. Sufficient unto this day are the segments you behold. The stone-paved road and intermittent series of steps ascend sharply, demanding exertion.

At intervals are a few of the 25,000 tall square watchtowers once reputed to dot the entire length of the Wall: Bleak bastions that could accommodate 100 watchmen each. Through their arches and windows the wind funnels relentlessly. Its howl is that of utter loneliness. A listener could imagine the lost voices of antiquity . . .

China was not China but a scattered series of feudal fiefdoms called the Warring States until a ruler named Shih Huang Ti came to power 221 years Before Christ. His dynasty, the Ch'in, gave China its name; his fear, of invasion from northern barbarians, gave the world one of its seven man-made wonders. Standardizing roads, money, language, laws and government service, improving agriculture, the emperor achieved a remarkable unification — and a need for security, especially from fierce nomads to the north.

Shih Huang Ti looked at a random series of fortifications scattered across the northern boundaries of his kingdom from the edge of Tibet on the west to the Gulf of Chihli on the east. These could be joined to create a formidable bastion against the alien invaders. Millions of men were mobilized to the labor. At one time probably one in every three able-bodied Chinese was either helping build, supply, or garrison the Wall. The death toll was staggering, and unrecorded except in legend and folk song.

The Wall they built, which other later workmen repaired during the Ming dynasty, varies from 20 to 40 feet

166

in height; over 30 feet wide; the road along its top accommodates five horsemen riding abreast. But figures do not prepare you for your initial encounter with the Wall. It is a presence, a signature of human ingenuity and labor set upon a hostile landscape.

But the wind, as you leave even as when you arrived, reminds you of crumbling portions of the Wall — out there in the distance — and of the transciency of all that humans build: Parthenon, Magino' Line, even this incomparable Great Wall.

In this world shrunken by instant communications systems and jet transportation, interlocked by mutual dependence on nature's resources and our own capabilities of self-destruction or survival, it is necessary that we try to know as much as possible and understand as realistically as possible what is happening in mainland China.

During my trip, there was surprisingly little reference (on the part of the Chinese with whom our group spoke) to the summer's devastating earthquakes. In Peking we were instructed not to take photographs of any of the damage or reconstruction. This was puzzling because such photographs would have shown (at least in the downtown and suburban areas we saw) the toilsome and effective rebuilding being done by a labor force relying on muscle power (women's as well as men's) more than machinery. Although the estimated 100,000 killed were in the area east of Peking, rubble and debris were still being brought under control in the capital by patient assembly lines of wheelbarrows as well as trucks; dwellings were being replaced by bricks and materials gathered in large part through the same grinding effort: All necessary to get as many quake victims as possible out of their fragile tents and thatched huts before bitter winter winds sweep down from Mongolia.

The national leader most identified with response to the catastrophe of the earthquake was Prime Minister Hua Kuofeng. If his name was largely unfamiliar to the 21 of us who entered China on Oct. 12 it was to become more familiar than our own names during the weeks that followed. As our U.S. Ambassador told us in Peking, midway through our visit, "You are in an extraordinary country at an extraordinary time."

In this short space it is impossible to present any full report of what we encountered, which was only the tip of the iceberg of political events in China. Mao's successor was chosen and Mao's widow and three associates were repudiated and arrested. But personal impressions of two significant events may be of interest.

First, our group was allowed to attend the mass rally held in Peking's famous Tien An Men Square on Sunday, Oct. 24. Considering the mammoth size of that square and the throng of more than one million it accommodated, it might seem that anyone who wished could have sneaked into the ceremonies. But in China one does not trespass lightly, and we clutched the green cards we were given that admitted us to a special section for "foreign visitors." There were, indeed, correspondents, observers, a crushing crowd from many countries of the world. We were placed between the monumental red and gold brilliance of the Gate of Heavenly Peace (a relic of the Ming dynasty), where the new Chairman and his associates stood, and the sprawling plaza jammed with a sea of people. Even the tall, heavy-set Hua Kuofeng was dwarfed by the panoply of his surroundings and the elevation of his imperious grandstand. Everything else was dwarfed by the stupendous numbers of people.

Driving through the city that Sunday morning, we had seen them gathering. On foot, marching in groups, in trucks, on bicycles they came, waving flags and brightly colored paper flowers, and always the pictures of Chairman Mao. The streets were moving tides of people. They parted reluctantly for a bus to move through, then flowed back together like waves after a ship has passed.

The music, as they marched and after they had gathered, was the martial, national music expected on such an occasion — dominated by the heavy, insistent beat of drums which seemed to pulsate with special force through the bright chilly afternoon air. And on every building around the Square, red flags whipped in the wind. Above the multitude, thousands of red flags held aloft by a host of hands rippled in the wind.

A voice crackled from the loud speaker. A translator told us that it was a summons to the people to "get themselves in order." Unbelievable as it seemed, quiet descended on that plaza. The stillness was impressive.

Hua Kuofeng did not speak. The editor of the Chinese paper explained to me that this would not be appropriate, for the rally was held to honor him. The mayor of Peking struck the theme for the "warm celebration" of Hua Kuofeng and "great victory over the Gang of Four." There were equally jubilant speeches by a representative of the Red Guards; by a chief engine driver, representing the workers; by a combat hero representing the army, and by a representative of the "poor and lower-middle peasants." The latter was a woman. Support of all these groups, especially the army, is essential to the new chairman's success.

From Peking, we went to Shanghai, China's largest city, and here we witnessed a second impressive political event: The eruption of giant posters, accompanied by large gatherings, parades and an atmosphere of general ferment. We had seen the "dazibao," or posters, elsewhere; here they dominated. Madam Mao, or Chiang Ching, and her radical nucleus were known as the "Shanghai Mafia." It was evident that if their arrest had aroused opposition anywhere it was here. Billboard-size cartoons depicted these alleged "traitors" as multi-headed serpents, as secret capitalists enjoying personal luxuries, as ugly demons. Posters with slogans and with long messages alike covered public walls, fences and even the corridors of some buildings. In a country where there is no other advertising, this outburst of denunciation and exhortation (how we longed to be able to read Chinese!) broke with special force. As people by the dozen or the hundred clustered to read these posters, we realized that they served a role as the people's newspaper. In fact, we learned that much of the early news to the world's wire services about the new government and the ousting of one faction had been gleaned from these posters . . .

Events taking place in China today are not only part of Chinese history; they will influence world history. It is a sobering experience to be present at their unfolding.

ONE ASPECT of the landscape of China, in countryside or metropolitan areas, that is most striking to a visitor from the West is the absence of advertising.

There are no billboards or signs describing the advantages or superiorities of one product over another. In the big department stores of major cities, or in the small shops which line the streets of all villages and cities, there are no posters or enticements pushing any particular line of wares.

It might be interesting to note here that if there were such commercial advertising it is unlikely that sex symbolism would be employed; China — at least publicly and officially — must be one of the most puritanical countries in the world today. The female figure is not displayed in any enticing or suggestive way, or at any stage of revealing undress, in the theater, in magazines or books, or in the nonexistent advertising. Only for ballet dancers, gymnasts and women athletes did any abbreviated costumes appear to be considered appropriate. Even in those movies we saw, the actresses' costumes were surprisingly modest.

This does not mean that there are no billboards or public signs on walls and buildings, however. The difference is in their purpose. In China they are the vehicles for messages from the government. They present quotations from Chairman Mao. They repeat the admonition and slogan, Serve the People. And they provide official news of special importance.

In certain squares of the larger cities and at junctions of some of the more heavily traveled thoroughfares and at public parks a gigantic billboard may suddenly punctuate the landscape. Often it displays a picture, in brilliant color, of a jubilant throng of young people engaged in some common endeavor, sometimes with their hands raised in a common forward thrust. At similar sites and along trails in scenic areas and on various buildings a vivid flash of Chinese characters, scarlet as a cardinal's wings, bears a thought of Chairman Mao. The Chinese may not be interested in advertising, but they know the uses of propaganda. Repetition is its essence.

The posters that Western visitors find so fascinating are unique. Usually they are simply large sheets of paper on which is written news or a message (often the two are the same) which officials have decided the people should know. These may cover fences, walls, or the sides of buildings,

171

or even be plastered along corridors in schools or public buildings if the news is of sufficient importance. And, in especially momentous cases, there may be pictures, political cartoons.

One block from our hotel in Shanghai, in a little plaza beside the river, stood one of the largest billboards we saw anywhere in the country. It was splashed with enormous caricatures of Chiang Ching (Madam Mao) and the so-called Gang of Four who had been placed under arrest just as we arrived in China. The "criticism," as their denunciation was officially called, was spelled out in words and pictures for the crowds that constantly gathered around these signs and posters. Newsmen from foreign countires find important clues about political upheaval and power struggles from these posters.

Quietly it sat in its glass cage, silent as the years stretching behind it — generations melting into centuries, centuries merging into ages, reaching back to beginnings of human civilization on the ancient earth.

What imagination has conceived this bronze vessel with its round, squat shape and three hollow triangular legs, and little mushroom-like decoration sprouting from the rim?

What hands had wrought the intricate designs?

What mind had devised the tools and vessels with which to blend the alloy of copper and tin into bronze and then fashion the mold in which this pot was cast?

For 3000, perhaps 3500, years it had withstood the ravages of age, gathering only the rich green patina which enhanced its beauty, and the destruction of savage wars.

172

It was a survivor.

October afternoon light, hazy with motes of dust, slanted through the windows of the museum in Shanghai. The soft, diffused sunshine, the quiet, deserted spaces of these rooms with their patient curators and guides were a startling contrast to the streets our group had just left.

The tree-lined streets of China's largest city were turbulent as a deep-running sea that day. People flowed through every thoroughfare and alley until it was difficult for a bus to move through the clogged passages. On bicycles, on foot, and in large military-type trucks they gathered for a parade that took place in mid-afternoon, then streamed back to the homes and surrounding countryside from which they had gathered. It was a political demonstration, warmly welcoming the new Chairman — revealing also, perhaps, some undercurrents of dissent which needed to be routed. From its noise and turmoil we entered the silent world of ancient art. Some might have thought our move a flight into irrelevance. Actually it was contact with a reality as vigorous and reliable as that surging around us — and strangely related to it, too.

The fertile basin of the North China plain, formed by the mighty Huang-ho or Yellow River, was the cradle of Chinese civilization. Here millet was first cultivated, nomads settled into villages, animals were domesticated, clay was shaped into pots, and a legendary chieftain called the Yellow Emperor welded a group of tribes into an alliance. With the rise of the Shang dynasty, from the 16th to the 11th Century B.C., the great Bronze Age came into being. Tools, weapons, cups, pots, beakers of bronze changed the nature of society. The technical excellence and artistic skill embodied in the great ritual vessels are astonishing and remain unsurpassed. They accompanied the rulers in their tombs, and it has been suggested that the bronze itself "was symbolic of the nourishing and maturing process within the earth."

173

The cycle that was to be repeated endlessly throughout the history of this land brought an end to the Shang rulers: Continuous wars weakened them, their oppression of slaves led to uprisings, and they were attacked by nomads from the northwest, the Chou. Although the King of Shang had a million troops who "came as fast as the wind with a noise like thunder," his forces were overwhelmed. Eventually, however, the culture of the conquered vanquished the conqueror. From the 11th Century to about 770 B.C. the Chou continued to create splendid bronzes. Not far from the Shang vessels stood an unusual oval bottle or canteen with flat sides and a rectangular base, boasting beautifully symmetrical designs. A Chou vessel for ordinary mortals, not for rituals.

A set of bells from the Chou dynasty also bore the ripe green patina of age on their heavily decorated surface. Since ancient Chinese bronze bells had no clapper, the tone was produced by striking the outer surface.

Mute, motionless, these examples of antiquity spanned time and space. The frets and fevers of the people of Shang and Chou and all those rulers who rose and flourished and in their turn fell, have long since faded from memory. But the art they wrought in bronze remains.

Quietly those bronze vessels and bells and rooms of artifacts remained washed in late afternoon sunlight as we left them behind and returned to the frets and fevers of Shanghai's streets.

Random observations and memories from explorations of China:

- How often our day started when *The East is Red*,

and frequently to the rousing notes of that national anthem. Yogurt served at breakfast, usually in little, blue, lidded porcelain cups, was delicious. So were the custard tarts we sometimes found. But the soup of rice and chicken broth, meat-filled pastries, and steamed bread which often seemed ready for the oven rather than the table, were less palatable at five-thirty and six in the morning.

• The head of a silk factory we visited wore the traditional Mao jacket, spoke all the proper lines of Party thought, and boasted of the progress of his industry and city. Then as we left one of us noticed the fingernail on this man's little finger. It was absurdly long and sharp as a claw. We remembered that in the old China of classes and status symbols, long fingernails had been the mark of the aristocrat, the scholar. How had this man working with machines and his Comrades each day managed to preserve a fingernail so long and vulnerable. And why? Did that one little idiosyncrasy negate some of the memorized speeches and forced allegiances?

• Who can forget the brightness of the children: their eyes, their shining faces, their clothes which are in sharp contrast to the dreary blue and grey and olive of adult clothing, and their dances. The vivacity of their dancing bears little relationship to the heavy titles of their presentations. Six little girls dance "The Barefoot Doctor Is A Good Auntie." Boys and girls join in a "Dance of Agricultural Knowledge." A paper flower dance is presented. Then five little girls perform a "Salute To The Martial Arts." There is a "Dance of Internationality" and one celebrating the "correct" building of a house. But the titles didn't matter as we watched the eager, beautiful children.

• The market in Peking was fascinating. Here was the daily life of the city partaking of such bounty as farms and meadows, rivers and sea afford. Clean, sunlit, vibrant with

175

color and noise, it was crowded. Live fish and fowls swam and strutted as they awaited hungry customers. Fruits and vegetables of many colors were arranged along great counters filling the sides of the long hall. Pork was the most expensive meat, with goose a close second and then chicken. Longest lines at the market were at the bean curd counter. Bean curd is an excellent source of protein,cheaper than meat, and is a favorite food across China.

• A retired doctor told us that the most effective means of birth control was late marriage. Therefore, China says it is best for girls to marry at age twenty-four or twenty-five; for boys, age twenty-seven to twenty-eight. Does this work? The doctor replied, "At present most of the youth answer the call to late marriage. In addition, the barefoot doctor goes to each house and discusses twice the family planning."

• Crops, plants, trees noted along the way: Rice in the South and wheat in the North, of course. Peanuts, sugar cane, sesame, cotton, corn, sweet potatoes. Bamboo. Pines and plane trees. Castor bean bushes.

• In Changsha the Lady Tai tomb, excavated in the early 1970's, is about 2000 years old. Surrounded by charcoal and white clay the tomb was sealed so effectively that the treasures of lacquer work and silk that were buried there are intact today. The body of Lady Tai was intact, too. She died about age fifty. She suffered from heart trouble, gallstones, and parasites. Some of the hair in her coffin was her own, some was a "hair piece" or wig. Although the discovery of the buried army at Sian outshone the unearthing of Lady Tai's three tombs, I felt closer kinship with the latter discovery. As we looked at some of the Emperor's figures which had been brought from Sian to Shanghai I marveled at their size, varied costumes and expressions, and their sheer numbers. But the silk banner in Lady Thai's tomb captured in its rich sweep of color and in its exquisite

176

detail the variety and energy of life. It was one of the most beautiful things we saw in China.

• The Yangtze River at Wuhan appears to be as wide as a couple of Mississippis. Its waters are brown and strong. The first bridge across the Yangtze was finished in the 1950's. We were told, "It united north and south." More than 3700 permanent construction workers were aided by many Wuhan volunteers. Earthwork approaches to the bridge were built by common laborers. Sometimes as many as 10,000 people labored on the bridge. And yet, many centuries earlier a wall, even more greedy of human life and stamina, was built across a much longer space. Of walls and bridges. What were their uses, what did they say about the societies that built them?

A wall. A bridge.

I return from China as I return from all explorations large and small, with a fresh awareness of home. And renewed perceptions of the traveler's lot.

"A traveler must have a falcon's eye, a donkey's ears, an ape's face, a merchant's words, a camel's back, a hog's mouth, and a stag's legs."

So says an old English proverb.

There are people who keep a coffee pot at a constant boil, ready for any unexpected visitor. There are those who keep the television turned on throughout the day and evening, ready for each immediate announcement of crisis or disaster. And there are individuals who keep a suitcase in constant state of preparedness, ready for any opportunity of exploration. I am one of the latter.

177

I find excitement and knowledge in visiting a mountain cove only a few hours' distant from my home; I relish the wonder of knowing a land and its people on the other side of the globe. Abroad in my own backyard or "across the waters" I try to remember wise old Samuel Johnson's remark: "The use of traveling is to regulate imagination by reality, and, instead of thinking how things may be, to see them as they are."

Whether or not I have the qualifications for travel that are listed above in the animals' characteristics, I have discovered that there are certain essentials for successful wayfarers. Not everyone possesses a measure of wanderlust. (Perhaps this is just as well; otherwise the world might resemble one immense beehive with drones and workers and an occasional queen swarming constantly to and fro.) If you do not yearn to seek out new paths and highways, listen to strange tongues, become familiar with different ways of thought and living, and if you are not prepared to pay a price in time and energy and resources for this exploration, then home is for you and you can bear witness to Shakespeare's sentiment, "When I was at home, I was in a better place."

But if there is a bit of the vagabond in you and you are going thirty or thirty thousand miles from home, there are choices to be made. They can determine the success or failure of your journey.

First, do you go alone or with others? It is true, as one English essayist has observed, that "Traveling in the company of those we love is home in motion." But if those we love are not available for the journey we might also reflect on astute Thoreau's counsel: "The man who goes alone can start today, but he who travels with another must wait til that other is ready." There seems to be a trade-off here between loneliness and freedom. The choice is yours.

178

Second, do we ramble to discover familiar comforts in new settings or to encounter the unfamiliar, receive the stimulation of difference? Two centuries ago Lord Chesterfield wrote in a letter to his son, "Those who travel heedlessly from place to place, observing only their distance from each other, and attending only to their accommodation at the inn at night, set out fools, and will certainly return so." To choose: why and how we travel.

And what luggage do we choose: stout hearts as well as stout shoes? Curiosity as well as toothpaste? A sense of humor as well as traveler's checks? Acceptance of happiness which must be carried from within before it will be discovered abroad?

Then there is Rediscovery of Home. An Italian proverb says: "Dry bread at home is better than roast meat abroad."

Englishwoman Frances Burney described a household inhabitant of 1782 who seems familiar in many households today. In one of her novels she wrote, "He seemed to consider his own home merely as an hotel, where at any hour of the night he might disturb the family to claim admittance, where letters and messages might be left for him; where he dined when no other dinner was offered him, and where, when he made an appointment, he was to be met with." Such a person's dwelling is merely a way-station between trips. It is not a home.

People of all countries have recorded in their folk sayings the true sense of what home means. A West African proverb asserts, "There is no home that is not twice as beautiful as the most beautiful city." And for the Spanish, "The smoke of a man's own house is better than the fire of his neighbors." An American saying shuns sentimentality but carries sentiment: "Even when you're looking for trouble, there's no place like home."

Sometimes travel brings us to a new home, a place more

compatible than we have known before. But whether root-bound or footloose, it is the capacity for enjoyment that will make us whole.

Edgar Allen Poe, who had a rare ability to arouse a sense of mystery and wonder through words, once said, "Odors have an altogether peculiar force in affecting us through association; a force differing essentially from that of objects addressing the touch, the taste, the sight or the hearing."

Summer is a season of potent and varied odors.

There are the smells born of weather: dust and dry grass and the acrid scent of the first big raindrops splashing in that dust when a summer storm descends. There is perfume of honeysuckle heavy in the evening twilight and of locust blooms drooping from boughs of tall trees along the highways.

There are the aromas of feasting: the pungent crispness of cool green cucumbers which have the freshness of the sea in their hearts; the redolence of cabbage; the milky luscious scent of fresh corn. As accompaniments, all the outdoor smells of smoke and broiling — juicy steaks and country ham and fish just taken from stream or lake. More delicate is the scent and taste of lemon and lime quenching the thirsts of summer.

Beds of mint, preferring cool, well-watered crannies, give off the refreshing odor of a spring morning. One stem crushed between your fingers banishes all staleness that may be corrupting the air, floods your nostrils with the very incense of nature.

Along the rows and borders of cultivated beds there are

the treasured fragrances of pampered roses and numerous lilies. Their sweetness is challenged by the piquancy of the geraniums and the spiciness of the marigolds. Like splashes of golden and orange fire the marigolds open their sunbursts — and as you cut a stem or crush a leaf they shed their strong and racy bouquet. Plebian they may be, but they leave their own signature in the air.

Mingling throughout the long full days of heat and sun and rain and storm are the scents of all the harvests of fruits. Beginning with the juicy sweetness of strawberries and the tartness of cherries reddening under the watchful eyes of the birds, the fruits fill these midyear months with the heavy ripeness of orange-meated cantaloupes and scarlet-centered watermelons, followed by the plump riches of plums and grapes. Under the limbs and vines where overripe plums and grapes nestle in the grass, there is a winy smell of sun and juice and sugars melting into earth, providing busy ants and a hundred insects with nectar.

And what odor is more characteristic of summer than that of newly cut grass, newly mown hay? Driving along an interstate with juggernauts of speed and power on every side, there comes an occasional breeze — drifting from one of the fields in the distance — of hay curing in the sun. It is a solace, a balm in the midst of frenzied haste and the stench of oil, gas, exhaust pipes.

As Edgar Allen Poe said, odors affect us through association. Lilacs stir memories of springtime past, of something good and gentle still surviving in the world. Smell of snow in the winter bespeaks a clear, clean world blanketed for a moment in silence and beauty. But the smell of grass on lawn or meadow, especially at early dawn or evening, is the very essence of summer's fragrance.

Several years ago my husband and I were visiting in Hollywood and we were invited to dinner one night at the home of a writer-producer who had been successful enough to acquire a house up one of the canyons where many of the well-known movie stars have lived. It was a charming place, neither as bizarre as some of the Moorish castle reproductions or Venetian villa fantasies built by characters whose money and imagination had both run wild, nor as coldly formal as some of the estates by which newly-rich kids from Bronx and Midwest whistle-stops were trying to build themselves background and prestige.

This was a house built with taste and decorated with style and used for living, not mere entertaining. But one room unnerved me completely. It negated everything else the house said.

There was a spacious dressing room which adjoined the wife's bedroom. It was a solid sheet of mirrors. Each of the four walls, from marble floor to a reflector-type ceiling, was an expanse of mirror. Along the length of one wall was a built-in dressing table and the top of this powder-and-perfume-laden creation was also a plate glass mirror.

The door which led into the bedroom was covered with a mirror. It was a room from which there was no escape from self. There could not even be a rest from self. I wondered at the woman who could want or enjoy such an inner sanctum. It occurred to me that this was the only room in the house without a window. And I wondered, do most of us live in a house of mirrors or of windows?

I still wonder. There are people who live all their lives surrounded by mirrors. They respond to everything that happens, from the catastrophe of war to a change in the weather, only as it affects their own small special affairs. They have compassion only for those who give them something in return — love, prestige, flattery. The dweller in the house of mirrors cannot respond to anything not reflected in his own physical comfort or intellectual self-satisfaction.

Those who live in rooms with windows, however, can look out. They see a world of wind and stars, sleet and sun, and other people. For them the mature realization is possible — the world is wide and the person who limits his vision to himself is cheating himself. For windows look out, but mirrors only reflect. And no matter how large the hall of mirrors, it is never spacious enough nor open enough to let in sunlight, the sound of others' voices, the sight of others' pain and pleasure. Worst of all, it permits no growth.

Probably my hostess that night in Hollywood had never heard the old Gaelic proverb, "The best mirror is a friend's eye."

Daylight disappeared gradually, dwindling across the quiet waters of the lake as surely as a bird in flight. And then it was gone, altogether vanished.

Darkness became deep and complete around us. Trees and shrubs that had shape and substance only a short while before were now only sentinels outlined against the sky. Paths were invisible. The only terrain we could see was that in the circumference of our campfire's light.

We sat around the campfire, speaking quietly — and not

at all, listening to the rasp of katydids and the falling waters of the nearby mountain stream as it rushed to join the lake in front of us. We felt the strangeness of our human voices, intruders in this wilderness where tall trees had grown for generations, the springs had sent forth their clear water for centuries, the earth had endured for eons. There was a sense of time different here than in the daily world we knew, a reminder and a pledge of eternity.

We were camping, as I had not done for many years, on Santeetlah Lake in the Nantahala National Forest southwest of the Great Smoky Mountains National Park. This is rugged, handsome country, home of black bear and deer and the famous Russian wild boar that were brought here from Europe many years ago and flourished in this congenial wild terrain. I was happy that we were able to find a campsite away from other people, for I must admit that when I am camping I am totally antisocial. I go to the city to discover people and one part of myself: The museums and theaters and concert halls, the squalid problems and the splendid promise of man's potential. I go to the woods to discover nature's messages, and myself; woods and water, moss and fern and lichen, insects, animals and birds.

The little plot we discovered for our camp was ideal to the point of being unbelievable. Before us stretched a wide expanse and inlet of Lake Santeetlah (beautiful Indian name), wooded down to the water's edge. Behind us a gentle slope separated us from the road's intrusion. At one side, surrounded by rhododendron and dog-hobble and ferns, was the brook where we washed our faces in the icy stream falling over mossy rocks. Above us was a canopy of trees: Hemlock, birch, poplar. And some thoughtful visitor ahead of us had left a small stack of firewood. It did not take long to accumulate a bed of red hot coals. The smell of wood-smoke blended with the bitter pungence of forest mulch to create

184

the essence of outdoor fragrance.

After we were in our tent, I could lie and watch the campfire. Just as I thought it was dying, a stick burned in two, one end blazing with a quick golden light. As this last flame died, the shadows crept back. I dozed, and when I looked again, only one single coal glowed out there in the night. I watched, listening to the summer sounds and the silence, aware of the distant glimmer reflecting from the lake. Then the last flicker of firelight snuffed out. Darkness engulfed us.

If there was a moment better than that of the campfire at night, it was the arrival of morning — shining and luminous as a pearl — and the aroma of woodsmoke and coffee and bacon while the mist lifted slowly from the lake.

If I could wish a gift for every family in this country at this tense and troubled time, it would be such an experience of camping together — and yet alone — in woods as nearly like a wilderness as possible. Perhaps there we may rediscover our sanity and civilization.

It struck suddenly — pain which made hand and arm and shoulder one excruciating universe of torment. To inhabit the kingdom of pain is to discover how thickly populated that world is.

For six weeks the agony of pinched nerves has been enough to provide the keepers of ancient dungeons and modern tortures with exquisite satisfaction. I have borne two children and had surgery and many of the common ailments that "natural flesh is heir to" in the past, but it is in the hidden, clutching, cruel constancy of this obstreperous nerve that I have encountered a real enemy.

My doctor friends have been excellent and able both as persons and physicians. I am a poor patient. I resist medicines (although I've been using my share recently) and I tend to believe that mind is stronger than matter (although the power of my positive thinking has been short-circuited during this current emergency).

The discovery that has astounded me most, however, has been learning how many friends and strangers have backs and shoulders and arms that bring them everything from occasional discomfort to regularly acute attacks of − well, the names are so numerous and so difficult to sort out and describe that we will only lump them together as hidden knots and traceways of suffering. I have always tried to understand and have compassion for others' feelings − whether of anguish or delight − but there is nothing like experience of one's own to permit us admission into the universality of pain.

The man who wrote, "He preaches patience that never knew pain," wins my hearty amen. Patience has never been my crowning virtue; I find it in especially short supply when I find someone who is offering it as consolation for others. Nature itself exacts from us great portions of patience; preach not of it to me.

The human rights doctrine that the United States has been enunciating is freedom from physical torture. In many countries of our 20th Century world agonies devised by humans to inflict on other humans are part of daily life reality, devices of political power secured by pain.

More than 1500 years ago St. Augustine observed that "The greatest evil is physical pain." Fourteen centuries later the English philosopher and jurist, Jeremy Bentham, agreed: "Pain is in itself an evil, and indeed without exception the only evil."

No one living in our modern world can fail to come to terms with the Nazi and Communist horrors that demonstrated the brutal capabilities of the human mind and heart. Those who can profit by or, let us face it, enjoy the pain of others, must be the most sick, the most evil among us. Every human has a right to be free of pain inflicted by fellow mortals. Each of us is frail enough, suffers enough, simply by bequest of our humanity. Surely our pain can create bonds, not bondage, to help our spirit rise free of our body's frailty.

My great-grandfather, my grandmother, my father, my mother, my husband: each had a green thumb, a green hand. Each was a gardener by hobby, by choice of pleasure. They were of different places, times, histories, temperaments — but they were akin by reason of their gift for growing things.

Gardening binds together the peoples of the world. It can put us in touch not only with the natural world but with our fellow humans as well. The garden as more than producer of food, as landscape and work of art, is one of our oldest traditions.

It has been said that "horticulture as the cultivation of plants for food and medicine in some kind of plantation is of Neolithic origin, and is therefore older than civilization and one of its basic elements." From this horticulture, agriculture probably evolved — and gardens were begun. Historians tell us that the inventors of gardening were almost certainly women.

The people of the Two Rivers, ancient Mesopotamians, were the first makers of gardens, which they emancipated "from purely economic purposes; the rich and mighty developed them into pleasances."

The Egyptians cultivated new species of plants — and laid down for the thousands of years of their own history and that of civilizations to come two very formal garden styles. One was the rectangle, and the other was the hillside terrace. Trees were held sacred.

China offered the natural scenery that Egypt lacked, and this influenced Chinese gardening. But in China gardening was an art. We are told that "some artists worked with paint on paper, some with ink on silk, and some with rocks and water and trees on a piece of land. Very often the painter, poet and garden designer were the same man, and a remarkably large number of great Chinese landscape painters were equally famous for their gardens. Chinese architects conceived of a house and garden as a unit. Rocks and water were the principal elements in creating a romantic landscape — in an art that survived for centuries and is now extinct.

It is surprising to learn that Greece did not cultivate a garden art until well past its cultural prime. Private gardens were not part of the design and construction of the cities. But sacred groves of trees were an important part of Greek culture, and under Cimon of Athens in the 5th century BC the first street trees in Europe were planted.

Arab culture had profound influence on the development of gardening in Europe. Water was the nucleus of the Islamic garden, as irrigation and ornamentation. The rose was the paramount flower, and fruit trees were of central importance. The charm of the Islamic garden is preserved for us today in Spain, in the cities of Seville and Granada, where the sound and sight and necessity of water is evident at every turn.

Italy, France, England — each contributed its own vision and innovations to our heritage of gardens. From all the past around the world we gather the seeds and the har-

188

vest, the art of gardening, and make it our own.

"Midway this way of life we're bound upon
I woke to find myself in a dark wood,
Where the right road was wholly lost and gone."

That dark wood of which Dante wrote awaits each of us. Sometimes it presents itself on a sunny summer afternoon. Before we even know the invitation has been issued the darkness gathers and we grope toward an ancient exploration.

Down, down into ourselves we go like a lost wanderer knowing no path through the woods, finding no light to illuminate the lonely way. We discover a self and a suffering whose existence is stranger than far countries or lost rivers.

No matter what age we may be by the calendar when the dark wood closes in, the moment comes at mid-life. Life on either side of the woods will never seem or be the same again.

Thus, within the space of an hour on a late June afternoon, I came into the dark woods.

I must tell of the beginning if the end is to have meaning.

On a Sunday morning in a long-ago-August Thomas Wolfe's sister brought a stranger to my house.

Thomas Wolfe was a big, exuberant writer who wanted to bring all of America into the grand design of his fiction. Mable Wolfe was a big, exuberant woman who wanted to bring all of her friends together in the generous embrace of her hospitality. And so, she came with the young stranger from Tennessee, unannounced, early one Sunday morning

189

while I was in the flower garden cutting a fresh bouquet before the dew disappeared.

I had a brand new degree from Northwestern University and the contract for a career to begin in New York in September.

But as my visitor and I talked — that day, and that evening, and the next day, and the next — we discovered that we were both interested in words and in woods, in theater and in thought, in being very social on some occasions and very much alone on other occasions. We were passionately fond of travel, and equally happy in staying at home. We liked the mountains and people up the little coves and hollows, and we also wanted to see deserts and cities and people who were in places of power and fame. Many of the things that made us perplexing to other people made us seem clear and right to each other.

From August to October was only a breath of time. Yet it was a lifetime. The contract and New York and September washed away in a misty haze. And on a brilliant blue autumn day, October 12, in the garden where I had been picking summer flowers, surrounded by banks of flaming leaves brought from the woods and baskets of great richly-colored dahlias and chrysanthemums, Mabel Wolfe's friend and I were married. And just to live up to the spirit of Thomas Wolfe, we took a wedding trip across America, from October 12 to December 20 — seeking to know our native land.

We remained married — to each other — for thirty-seven years. I pity those who will never know such a long and good togetherness. It was not easily achieved. Courage, effort, generosity, humor, determination went into those years. The result was love.

Then, on an afternoon in June, sun-tanned and smiling, suddenly he sank onto the grass beside his garden and was dead.

The world was changed. For a few people on this mysterious planet nothing will be the same again. Yes, the oak outside the window will stand, the garden will bear, summer will flourish and wane, other lives will continue their familiar routine — but all diminished because he is not here. And I shall continue, too, diminished by his absence, but better than I could ever have been without his presence for a little while.

We met in a garden and we parted in a garden. I was picking flowers in my mother's garden in Asheville on that summer morning when we met. He wore a white shirt, open at the collar with rolled-up sleeves, against which his smooth skin was a golden tan and his eyes were the clear blue of sea or sky, and before that day was finished he had asked me if I liked books and the woods and the final question — Beethoven. Two weeks later I canceled my career in New York. In October we were married. I believe there never was a couple more destined for each other.

Very few people knew the true dimensions of James' life. In a world where outer appearances are judged as reality he invested more and more of his time in inner riches. In a time when bigger is considered best and power seems a prize worth any sacrifice, he cherished the fragile spirit, the delicate creativity that flows from an eternal power. In a period when the loud and the self-proclaiming receive the world's awards, he was quiet and self-forgetful.

He was also a person of immense power. With all his gentleness he was capable of deep anger. Anger against injustice — injustice in any form or dimension — led him into some lonely valleys. He never talked of those experiences because he had no martyr's complex — too much laughter to be a martyr. And when his family or friends or society caught up with his farsighted vision, he never suggested an attitude of "I-told-you-so." He was too busy looking ahead to other horizons. In all his patience he seethed with powerful impatience. Impatience with trivia — the second-rate in our cultural, spiritual, educational, political, industrial, individual and social lives — led him to some lonely pinnacles. This grieved him because any riches of mind or spirit or body that he discovered he wanted to share with everyone else. And every day was an adventure of discovery for him.

I never met anyone who savored more deeply the potential of the moment. Whether we were in a strange land or here in our own familiar mountains, whether we were listening to the first katydids of summer or the Eroica Symphony, whether we were among exciting famous people or talking with old-timers or were alone together. To whatever we were doing he brought full appreciation, passion, imagination.

People sometimes asked if he was disconcerted by my writing, my career. How little they knew him! He had no identity crisis, no need to narrow anyone else's life to enhance his own. Indeed, one of the purposes of his life seemed to be to make sure that everyone — no matter race or sex, social status or creed — should have not only opportunity but encouragement to be not only good but best.

And he was the best. Funny and sad, uniquely innocent and infinitely sophisticated, he balanced the world of nature and the world of books and dwelt in a realm of special goodness. He would not have liked that word, it would embarrass him. But he was good. We shall rarely see his like again.

A week ago he left on one of the few journeys we have not taken together. But he is not wholly away — and I am not wholly here. We are still together.

Crossing America's Great Divide still imparts a sense of adventure. Preparation for it may be made by awareness of the passages across the Appalachians that lead from the watersheds emptying into the Atlantic Ocean and those that flow into the Gulf of Mexico. That, too, is a moment that can kindle the imagination, offering us the view eastward and westward.

But it is the route through and over the towering barrier of the Rocky Mountains that is the ultimate experience of geographic division in the land: Division and unity as well.

Today marks the anniversary of a Great Divide in my life. And if I have learned anything during the past year it is that everyone makes this journey at some time in his/her life. Of course, I knew this in my mind long ago. I even found my way through a number of lesser barricades, as each of us must. But the past year's journey has brought the common experience of our human condition into my blood and bone, into my heart and memory, as well as into my mind.

Often, now, as I look at family members or friends or strangers who share part of their life with me, I find myself repeating a phrase over and over in my mind: The walking wounded. They may be laughing — or quiet. They may be plunging into activity — or retiring from it. They may be reaching out — or dipping inward. But they have traversed the Great Divide.

My husband and I once crossed the Rocky Mountain Divide in winter. Snow crusted the highway and rose in giant banks on either side until the highway resembled a country lane more than a national thoroughfare. Dark evergreens, their boughs weighted with heavy burdens of snow, arose on either side. There was no other traffic. The road wound upward, in a silent, lonely world. In the high, clear air our surroundings seemed at once strange and familiar, beautiful and forbidding.

The pass itself was not especially remarkable. There was simply an interval between one watershed and the next, between one landscape and another that would succeed it. Having made the crossing, however, there was a deep, a penetrating awareness that a change had been experienced; this was the same — and yet a different — world. This was what many of the early westering pioneers must have felt as they toiled over these mighty walls. In a sense, it is what each of us knows as we struggle through the wilderness that inevitably rises before us, surrounds us, permits no other passage.

My encounter with the invisible Great Divide began not in winter snows but in last summer's greening garden. Without a hint of warning death removed my campanion traveler and left a strange and lonely road to be explored. In those high passes it is devastating to look back, it is cruel beyond bearing to look forward. The journey itself becomes, for the moment, all that can be borne.

Each of us, alone, crosses that divide. Yet we are not alone. Together we share the human tragedy and comedy. The wounds become scars of living badges of caring, symbols of participation in life.

Four o'clock in the morning. Four o'clock at night. It

is the witching hour.

Wolves prowl in the darkness. Now they come from the corners where they lurk during the day; they emerge from the shadows that have sheltered them during the evening. These are not the wolves with shining pelts and gleaming eyes and a loping gait that carries them across barren wilderness. These are the wolves that roam the blackness silently. Their presence abolishes sleep. Their name is loneliness.

In the silence of four o'clock the difference between aloneness and loneliness is profound. To be alone is not necessarily unpleasant. For creativeity to function at its highest level — from physics to poetry, from music to home-making — a certain amount of solitude is necessary. For a child to become an adult and for an adult to grow into a sensitive, fulfilled human being it is essential to spend more time with one's self. Of all the "advantages" offered people today, especially children, this is one of the most neglected. With all our organized activities, there is precious little time (or should we say little precious time?) left for being alone.

But loneliness is something different. It preys upon those who have been happiest, loved deepest, made the most profound commitments. Circumstances change. Life's realities stalk the wild game and the tame alike and we all become the quarry. Suddenly those who have helped shape each day's dimensions, those who have shared a moment's delights or a decade's anguish — are gone. Inevitably, irretrievably, they are gone. Those left behind may or may not be alone but they are abruptly, subtly, cruelly vulnerable to loneliness.

It may attack in the most crowded room or along the busiest street.

It my pounce without warning at the sound of a certain bar of music or the simple sight of a man and a woman holding hands.

It may strike with advance notice, upon a certain anniversary or holiday, or without warning during the most improbable experience.

It may nibble at the memory and cause only an ache in the throat or it may tear at the mind and wrench flesh and muscle with the pain described in no doctor's book, defined in no medical manual.

Above all, the darkest hours of the night/morning belong to loneliness. And the wolves, once unloosed, do not submit easily to restriction. They pad through the lightless hours with infinite patience. Only their victim can recognize them — or banish them.

Four o'clock in the morning. The loneliest hour on earth.

I cried last week.

One of the experiences I have not yet learned to cope with in a reasonably satisfactory manner during the past year and a half is listening to music.

By music I do not mean the noise that is playing havoc with our ear drums and our nerves, and I do not mean the easy tunes and lyrics that come and go as casually as chickens' clucking. I mean the sounds that reflect the human spirit and inspire it with a renewed sense of the wonder and potential of life.

I heard a Mozart symphony and I was reminded of long-ago afternoons in a little stone house in the mountains when James and I listened to the magic wrought by Toscanini as he interpreted the genius of the master composers, or as we participated in presentations from the Metropolitan Opera on Saturday afternoons when "the great gold curtain" lifted on the golden voices of singers gathered from many lands to share musical revelations of the joys and sorrows of life. I remembered the total experience of listening to records with someone who felt music to the marrow of his bones and the depths of his being. The rhythm that served him well in tennis and other sports, the mathematical talents that astonished and pleased professors, these were part of his understanding of music. Through that sharing I came to hear music as I had never heard it before.

I also came to understand why many people resist listening to this level of music. It awakens the mind. It stirs emotions. It engages the spirit. Most of us find it too demanding to be moved out of our familiar routines. We deny the challenges that require us to care, to cry or to laugh.

Last week I cried. I am not ashamed to admit it. Music lifted me into a realm of memory and imagination that made me wish we could never die, and reassured me that perhaps we never do.

Two centuries ago a Polish king observed that "Laziness is premature death." Perhaps, then, we are often prematurely dead: When we fail to reach out to seize not only the good or the better but the best; when we label something "low brow" or "high brow" and thereby deny ourselves one whole realm of experience; when we cease to open our ears and eyes, our minds and hearts, to the capability of suffering and pleasure – and the curious ways in which they may sometimes be intertwined.

We need more of humanity's great music to enrich and ennoble our lives. To deny it is to bring one kind of premature death a little closer – for ourselves and for civilization.

I have cried but the tears were of joy and riches remembered.

197

From a wide variety of conversations I brought home one nugget. Like most wisdom, it seems transparent in its simplicity. Each new pondering unfolds deeper layers of meaning. The man to whom I was listening said, "The opposite of love is not hate; the opposite of love is fear."

Consider how true this is in many areas of our life. Except for a pathological minority among us, we are not being dishonest or hypocritical when we say, as white people, that we do not hate black people, or when we say, as blacks, that we do not hate whites; what we do feel — too often, in the inner depths of our being — is fear of one another.

It is sometimes suggested by critics of our society that this affluent country hates its poor, its unsuccessful, its rejected members. And we would probably be correct in our denial of hatred; we simply fear them. We fear the demands they make on our comfort, our platitudes, our conscience.

There has been an assumption by some commentators on the current scene that the "generation gap" has deteriorated into hatred in some quarters. And sometimes it does seem that the intensity of youth's rejection of older leadership, and the vehemence of middle-aged reaction to young questioning, borders on hate. But fear is a much more accurate diagnosis. An older generation is fearful of the change demanded by youth, and that youth is fearful of the power of an older hierarchy to block or qualify change.

Consider in our personal lives how few of us have the inclination — or energy! — for hate, and yet how often our thoughts are addled and our actions are ennervated by fear. And sometimes it seems that those who possess the most in physical strength and goods are the most fearful of all.

Psychologists have told us of the deadly toll that hate can make on health and personality. Hate corrodes all that it touches. The toll of fear is no less dreadful, only less sharp, more gradual. Fear erodes all that is constructive and affirmative. That is why any leader, at the smallest domestic level of a parent in the home or the highest level of national political office, who uses fear as a lever, a tool, a weapon, an advantage, is betraying the best and healthiest in individual or national character.

Fear destroys all that love of a person, family, nation, or humanity can build. Civilizations have been destroyed by fear and the apathy and oppression which accompany fear. Yes, my friend made me a lasting gift when he reminded, "The opposite of love is not hate; the opposite of love is fear."

Visiting in a friend's home recently, I was attracted by several unusual items displayed on a small table in the library. One was an antique Roman coin, rich and handsome in design. I was reminded of a verse I once read:

"All passes, art alone
Enduring stays to us;
The bust outlasts the throne,
The coin, Tiberius."

The Romans themselves recognized that truth, of course.

One of them adapted the saying, "Art is long, and life short," from the longer observation by Hippocrates, the Greek father of medicine, who said, "Life is short, art long, opportunity fleeting, experience treacherous, judgment difficult."

The question, of course, is not whether we can personally attend every exhibit at the gallery or every concert by the symphony; the question is whether these organizations shall continue to exist and flourish and reach out to new audiences of the young, and others who have not had previous experience of these arts, and whether or not they shall become a part of our civic and regional life.

When we open our ears to music and our eyes to painting, sculpture, design, we begin to emerge from a smaller world into a larger universe. As the great French novelist, Romain Rolland, once wrote in a letter to an American musical society: "In the field of art there is not − there should not be − any rivalry among nations. The only combat worthy of us is that which is waged, in every country and at every hour, between culture and ignorance, between light and chaos. Let us save all the light that can be saved!"

The combat between "culture and ignorance, between light and chaos" is not always as clear-cut as contests on a battlefield or playing-ground. And as Rolland said, it is continuing − never completely won, never totally lost. It is, however, one effort that brings us pleasure, satisfaction − even joy − all along the way.

"Let us save all the light that can be saved!"

They stand, on a desk at my mother's home, bookends which afford me both pleasure and regret. At an auction at

Parke-Bernet Galleries they would not bring any impressive price. Yet they are of inestimable value to me.

Two simple pieces of wood, carefully fashioned and polished, a rich, light golden in color with a dark, chocolate-brown wave down the middle, as if some young girl's living hair had been momentarily captured in all its cascading variety. The grain of the wood invites a touch, an almost involuntary stroke to share in this rare wave-like pattern.

These bookends are of ancient origin, from an irreplaceable source, They were created from the heart of one of the largest, oldest yellow poplars ever recorded in Southern Appalachia or America. Expert accounts of its size and age vary. In a volume, *Trees of the Southeastern United States,* published in 1937, there is reference to "the Reems Creek poplar" in Buncombe Couunty, N.C. "It was 198 feet high and 10 feet, 11 inches in diameter, four feet above the ground. It was probably the largest tulip tree (or "yellow poplar") in the world. The tree was estimated by Harvard experts to be 1000 or more years old."

A more romantic account gave this description: "Back about 889, when Alfred the Great was pushing things around in Wessex, a tender young poplar sprout pushed its way through covering vegetation at the head of Reems Creek. Then, for more than 10 slow rolling centuries, it grew until it achieved the rating of the largest deciduous tree in the world, towering some 200 feet high."

The forest king loomed above the virgin timber which surrounded it and attracted scientists to study it as well as local admirers to stand in awe before its giant trunk beneath its leafy boughs. Then, one April morning in 1935, a mountain man living in the vicinity saw smoke rising from the woods in the neighborhood of the big tree. When he reached the site he found that campers had spent the night in the hollow base of the tree and they had failed to extinguish

201

their fire when they departed.

Local people used some of the wood from the remains. One had more than a thousand board feet sawed. He later described the wood: "That's curly poplar. Ain't no more of that! You'll see curly maple, curly birch, or curly walnut, but curly poplar — you jest don't see it."

No, the likes of the Reems Creek poplar will not be seen again. A thousand years were needed to grow the tree which could be destroyed overnight by indifferent campers. But holding the bookends made from one small segment of the poplar's body it is good to contemplate the sweep of centuries, the flow of animal and bird and plant life, the cycle of seasons which were part of this life. Such a link with nature's immortality has value beyond easy assessment.

When did it happen?

At what moment by the clock or which date on the calendar did the summer reach its zenith and turn toward autumn?

Was it the first night we heard the katydids?

Their voices were muted at first and minor in number. We had to listen carefully: Was it really a katydid, or some other midsummer insect grating its own special music? Then it came again, unmistakable this time. And within a few evenings the shrubs and trees were full of their sounds . . . time was passing.

Was it the first morning we heard a bluejay cry with a special sound of the "high lonesome" against the clear blue sky? There had been the songs and chirps and calls of many various birds throughout the rushing spring and busy summer, but this was a different sound, familiar and haunting, reminding those full of remembrance that the seasons turn and that a bird flashing through the luminous air can identify the year's progress.

Was it the first afternoon we walked on a patch of lawn and heard the sound of leaves underfoot?

There is a tree which always sheds early. It stands at one edge of our backyard, and like some people it invariably seems to be in a hurry to herald deaths and departures. While summer's lemonade and watermelons are still being enjoyed under its branches, its leaves start sifting down in premature haste. Suddenly one day there is the rustle of withered leaves under our hot-weather sandals and the smell of dry leaves mingling with summer's marigolds. They turn our thoughts toward fall.

And so it arrives once more. Suddenly. Before we had realized summer was well under way. Autumn.

There is a slightly different slant to the sun. The shadows have a depth we did not notice during previous days.

There is another texture to the grass and plants, a toughness which was missing in spring's lush tenderness only recently.

There is a variation in the noontime's heat and the nighttime's chill; the heat still sharp and intense but somehow less oppressive, shorter lived, than it was only a handful of days ago, and the chill more pronounced, more prolonged.

Somewhere, at some hidden moment, some unheralded zenith, summer reached its pinnacle and the earth turned toward autumn. No almanac needs to tell us what we can read with our own senses — our own melancholy, nostalgic awareness of the earth.

Do you believe parents are kind to children when they make life as easy as possible? ("I don't want my children to grow up the way I did. I want them to have it 'better.' ")

Do you believe friends are good to us when they make no demands? ("I want them to like me.")

Do you believe employers are thoughtful when they maintain no special standards, require no effort at improvement? ("It's too much trouble to get anybody to do his best.")

My own answer to those questions is in the memory I have of two teachers. I call them Miss Tanner and Mrs. Dixon, because those are not their real names. Everything else about this little fable is true, however.

Each of the 15 or so students in my grammar school class looked forward to the day when we would enter Mrs. Dixon's room. And each of us dreaded the moment when we might be assigned to Miss Tanner's grade.

Mrs. Dixon was a short, plump lady who wore pastel colors — the blues matched here pretty round eyes, the pinks accented here clear, fine skin. Her hair was always beautifully arranged and she spoke with soft, endearing tones. Studies under her were supposed to be pleasant and easy and she was not stingy with high grades on themes and exams.

Miss Tanner was somewhat different. She was not very tall but seemed taller because of her angular figure. Straight brown hair often hung limply beside her weathered face, and the grays and browns she favored in her clothes did nothing to improve her attractiveness. She smelled of cold cream and camphor.

But we would have overlooked the difference between blue dresses and brown, we would have overlooked the cold cream and the firm voice, if it hadn't been for the high standards of performance set by Miss Tanner. Why, she had been known to "keep in" a student who hadn't learned to spell or multiply correctly — until he learned the problem or the word! And she made everyone earn the grade he or she received.

I went through both their classes. And I loved Mrs. Dixon. She was so easy to love: Complimentary, cheerful, charming. At the end of the year I took her a present: A box of rose-scented dusting powder and I almost cried because I was leaving her room.

When I finished Miss Tanner's class I took her no gifts. I had liked her well enough, but there was a feeling of release in leaving her keen eye, sharp ear, questioning tongue. I had worked harder than I had ever worked in any previous class of my school years.

And yet . . .

As I entered high school, I began to find gaps in my knowledge, many of which should have been covered during my studies with Mrs. Dixon. And I began to use the facts and habits I had acquired under Miss Tanner. When I went on to college, I still encountered deficiencies and proficiencies which I could trace back to these two teachers.

My memory of Mrs. Dixon and of Miss Tanner has enlarged my understanding of what each of these women represented.

Their legacy to me is knowledge of the fact that — easiest is not always best.

I wish I could give Miss Tanner a box of dusting powder.

Silence.

That is the first impression and the lasting memory of the vast wilderness, at once inviting and forbidding, known as the Okefenokee Swamp in Southeastern Georgia. The silence is that of centuries, time moving here at a pace unfamiliar to frantic human schedules, slowly accumulating and destroying. The silence is that of nature, an intricate web of life in which plants and animals, land and water, compose a pattern of co-existence as delicate as a cobweb, as tough as an alligator's hide. The silence swallows the noises of the 20th century and seems to remind us of the ultimate silence of space beneath and beyond the earth itself.

Although 681 square miles embrace an impressive chunk of real estate, Okefenokee is one of the smallest wilderness areas in the National Wilderness system. But its complex of islands, lakes, forests, prairies and jungles provides an experience of variety not matched by many larger refuges. I was reminded again of the fact that many times we journey far afield to enjoy wonders that we have neglected to discover closer at home.

To go from the Great Smokies to Okefenokee is not a long distance in space but it seems to span a chasm of difference. As the Smokies are piled up and scooped out in towering pinnacles and plunging valleys, the sweep of Okefenokee is leveled and watery. The swamp has been called a "child of the retreating Atlantic," for it was born more than 250,000 years ago when the ocean lay some 75 miles inland from its present Georgia coast. A basin formed by a sandbar became a shallow lagoon and as the ocean gradually receded the lagoon drained, the sand basin became the bed of a swamp, and the headwaters of the Suwannee and St. Marys Rivers, this mysterious botanical paradise, was formed.

"Land of trembling earth," the red men called it. That is the meaning of the strange word, Okefenokee, that it took Europeans and white Americans a century or two to spell and pronounce. It is a name both beautiful and precise. As one naturalist has described it, "The swamp is actually an immense slow-running body of water held in a shallow basin of sand, and impeded by congregations of cypresses, by vast areas of sphagnum moss, by dense thickets of shrubs and by islands thronged with pines." Entering the swamp by boat, threading the quiet, narrow waterways, or by wooden walkways built out into the thickets, the visitor immediately becomes part of a world that seems prehistoric in its tall cypresses, festoons of Spanish moss, and strange carnivorous plants – and in its guardians, the alligators. As they glide through the waterways or lie sunning on the grassy hummocks, they seem both menacing and marvelous – reminders of the age of dinosaurs. Alligators are symbolic of the great swamp itself: Ancient yet pulsing with life, quiet yet possessing potential for danger.

People have been a part of Okefenokee's long history, too. It has offered refuge to a wide variety of roamers and settlers: Indians (Creek and Seminole, the latter led by the fiercest chief, Billy Bowlegs, who held out longest against the U.S. Army here in the Okefenokee), deserters from various wars and Army rolls, black slaves fleeing to freedom, lumbermen and turpentine workers, farmers and hunters, and even dreamers-of-empire who attempted to drain the swamp.

Now they are gone. Okefenokee remains the domain of white ibis and bear, bobcat and knobby-kneed cypress,

207

pitcher plant and great blue heron, cottonmouth and rattle-snake and grey lichen. And silence.

As one visitor observed, "In the Okefenokee, man is subdued. The sound of earth overwhelms his voice and tells him that in the long haul he moves to its music. Nature, in the end, simply does not heed man's rules. If that truth is not demonstrable now, then we have lost sight of the meaning of our occupancy of this planet."

When we consider riches which may be part of our personal, regional, national or human inheritance, we tend to think of houses and land, minerals and objects of art, things. But a living, indispensable treasure we often forget is our heritage of language.

Words are weapons, tools, instruments of communication between the past and the future, which set us apart from all other creatures on this earth. They are not static. Their meaning changes; their usage declines or increases. They are distorted into propaganda or they are polished into truth. They are our language.

One of the interesting features of language is dialect. A person of Irish, English, Scotch or American background may be considered "English-speaking," but each may be distinguished from the other more readily by speech than by manner or appearance. In our own country, a Yankee from Maine and a Midwesterner from Indiana and a mountaineer from Southern Appalachia may have cars and clothes and television programs that are just alike, but their speech is distinctive.

Anyone who is ashamed of a native speech should remember the words of the great Irish poet, William Butler Yeats. "No dialect is ugly," he said. "The bypaths are all beautiful. It is the broad road of the journalist that is ugly . . . It is only from them (peasants or country folks) one could learn to write, their speech being living speech, flowing out of the habits of their lives, struck out from life itself."

Much of the vitality of the American language arises from what we might call its illegitimacy. Born of many nationalities and adaptations, it incorporates the rich variety of our ancestry. And nowhere is that vitality or variety more evident than in the language of our Southern mountains. Words long since discarded in their place of origin may be alive and current here; adaptations of other words mint fresh terms of us. Consider, for instance, the genealogy of some of our dialect.

From the Scotch and Irish we have stingy, canny, uncanny, hemlock, queer, shoddy, shucks, spree, shunt; and solely from the Irish come brogue (shoe), let on (pretend), drugget (carpet), jaw (impudent talk), thick (intimate) and going on (making fun).

Here we have kept some of the 17th Century pronunciations which were long since abandoned in England, from whence they came. Among these we might recognize "critter," "varmint," "pizen," "ketch," "obleeged," and "hanted." If mountain people, especially of an older generation, say "afeard," "fleshy," "chore," "poor" (lean) or "allow" (affirm), who is to say that they are not using English properly? They are only going back to an earlier time.

It is also well to acknowledge our indebtedness to the speech of various Indian tribes, not only for the melodic names of many of our rivers, states and mountains (Mississippi, Wyoming, Allegheny), but also for names of many plants and animals and implements. Among these are opossum, skunk, raccoon, terrapin, hickory, persimmon, squash,

209

hominy, succotash, tapioca, canoe and tomahawk.

The French in America left their linguistic influence in many words: Prairie, rapids, bayou, chowder, picayune, levee, chute, caribou and shanty. And the Spanish bequeathed us calaboose, palmetto, pewee, barbecue, stampede, canyon, coyote, lariat, sombrero and adobe. From Holland we received such words as coleslaw, stoop, cookie, waffle, pit (of peach or cherry) and Santa Claus. And the Germans gave us pretzel, delicatessen and hamburger!

Of our bequests from many languages, and of our regional dialects within this country, we may be proud. Appreciation of this legacy invites us to more awareness in our use (and misuse) of words.

A month of exploration across France with a couple who have friends and favorite byways from Paris to the Pyrenees.

I was hesitant about being the odd third one on a long journey, a travel role I hadn't played before, but I was put at ease by their generous reassurances that our car was larger and more comfortable because of my sharing, that my readiness to laugh rather than rage at inconveniences made daily details more fun, and that we enjoyed a similar interest in the history of any person or place we visited. When we returned home we were still friends — after ventures and adventures in village inns, as house guests of French friends they have known for many years, as explorers of peaceful country lanes and clamourous thoroughfares.

What happened during those weeks? Many non-momentous but memorable occasions and encounters.

We ate croissants still hot from the oven of a village

bakery at four o'clock in the morning on our way to greet sunrise on the Normandy beaches. As daylight spread over deserted Omaha Beach we listened to the sea lapping against the shore like the murmur of voices from row after row of white crosses on the green meadow atop the steep cliffs. It was an hour for remembering.

In addition to the usual sauces and French gourmet way with food, we savored fresh fruits served simply at the end of each dinner. From one friend's small, walled-in city garden we ate luscious boysenberries, two varieties of strawberries, red raspberries, and the juiciest, sweetest of white peaches tinged with a rosy blush — all these ripe at the same time. And at country inns we discovered robust cassoulet, the rich dried bean casserole with pork or goose or duck, cooked for many hours, nourishing and satisfying.

We marveled at the color and character of Toulouse Lautrec's paintings in the museum devoted to his life and work in the picturesque town of Albi, and marveled again later as we followed detailed depiction of the Norman Conquest captured on the one and only Bayeux Tapestry, the only tapestry I ever found truly appealing or beautiful.

We drove above clouds in the steep, green countryside of the Pyrenees, and plunged into the cross-section of humanity swarming over Andorra's clotted streets where everything is on the market — from fresh meat to old gold, from Cointreau to fake coins.

We explored the Roman roots of Nimes, the orchards and fields of Provence, and discovered that governments are for the most part unpopular everywhere. A ditty in southern France:

"Parliament, Mistral, and Durance

Are the three scourges of Provence."

Mistral is the fierce wind that sometimes afflicts the region. Durance is the river that may become in spring a raging torrent. And Parliament — well, Parliament is Parliament.

We were reminded once again that violence is not some phenomenon new to our time or nation; the blood of centuries of religious conflict, royal intrigue, economic privilege, military power, underprivileged revolt, soaks the earth and ancient thoroughfares of Europe.

And we joined generations of other travelers who have had cause to thank Napoleon for at least one legacy: the trees he caused to be planted along the highways and roads of France to provide shade for his soldiers. Under several of those trees we paused, had fresh crusty bread and sharp cheese and wine and fruit, and were refreshed.

For anyone who has had a lifelong romance with grapes a journey across France in the late summer and early autumn can become a heady experience.

Is there any design in nature more full, graceful, and resplendent than that of a cluster of grapes? They may come in many shades but I always think of them as rich and royal purple, fat with juice, hanging in a series of curving lines and topped with green leaves and tendrils that trail from brown stems like stray wisps from a lavish coiffure. Is there any taste more opulent than that of the juice of the grape, fresh or fermented?

The various provinces of France boast their own distinct varieties of grapes and vintages of wine. Most famous to Americans, perhaps is the champagne country of the valley of the Marne. Vineyards flourish like patchwork quilts along the slopes and in the fields beside this beautiful river. None

212

is more famous than those of Moet & Chandon, home of Dom Perignon, the champagne named after the monk who experimented with "marrying" wines from a number of different grapes and thus created the "bubbly" known around the world.

Jean-Remy Moet, grandson of the founder, was a friend of Napoleon and today, in the firm's museum-reception room, the Little Emperor's tricorn hat and one of his traveling chests is on display. Menus from famous occasions during two centuries are also interesting to read; each features a Moet & Chandon wine, of course.

Less grandiose in surroundings and history but equally interesting to me was a visit to vineyards quite distant from the champagne country. In southern France, a few miles north of Avignon, is a village called Chateauneuf-du-Pape. Here, at the beginning of the 14th century, when the popes moved their headquarters from Rome to Avignon during the century of the Great Schism, they also built an imposing summer residence on a hill overlooking the Rhone River valley. Today only a skeleton of the massive castle and its ramparts still stands, but the view this site commands is still there for a visitor to enjoy. It is a view of red tile roofs on houses clustered along the hill and of vineyards stretching away to the river, covering the nearby slopes.

Chateauneuf-du-Pape is not only the name of a palace and a village; it is best known as the name of an excellent red wine. A young man who is himself the grandson of a founder of one of these wine producers introduced us to his home and business and history. First, he showed us the land that produces these special grapes. In fact, it was not land we saw but stones — for the unique fact of these vineyards is that they are planted in fields so stony that it seems there is no soil to nourish roots. Underneath the small round rocks, worn and smoothed as if by centuries of running water, there is dirt — its heat and moisture supposedly conserved by the layers of stones above.

Some 320 individual owners tend the vineyards of this area. Each phase of growing and picking the luscious grapes, crushing and distilling their juice, requires much careful labor by hand. The acres tended by our young host were first planted by his grandfather. Neither his father nor his uncles were interested in work on the land — but the dedication of this grandson to this place, its fruits, its special product was an excellent thing to see. His devotion to his grandfather was evident in all that he said. When he introduced us to his pretty wife and small son at the entrance to the chateau near the winery his devotion to the younger generation was equally evident.

In every country it is good to know that there are those working in the old tradition of excellence, appreciating the earth, and its fruits.

I have been to Carcassonne again.

One morning a dozen years ago a husband, two young sons, a mother, and I crossed the Aude River in the Midi, or southwestern part of France, and looking up from the bridge beheld a medieval city hanging against the blue sky like a dream of distant kingdoms in a Brueghel painting or the fantasyland of a Disney movie, like all the imaginary kingdoms of childhood and knights in armor. It was the ancient fortress of Carcassonne we were discovering and an exciting moment turned into a happy visit within a living museum of awesome proportions.

A few days ago, in the good company of a couple who

have friends living in Carcassonne, I returned. Memories flooded back — but new experiences provided fresh memories to merge with the older ones. The immense stone walls and towers, the cobbled streets and winding alleys, the colorful little squares, the bustling shops and imperturbable medieval buildings — these lay swaddled in early morning fog or bathed in the light of a full moon as I walked during some of the hours when the daily throngs of visitors had departed through the great old gate across a drawbridge. This most authentic depiction extant of ancient and medieval fortifications must please the French people themselves for they made up the bulk of those discovering La Cité, as this historical town is called. The "modern" lower city is beside the river while this storybook re-creation sprawls on the hill which towers above it.

I looked back to my notes of an earlier time and refreshed my history. The Old Cité of Carcassonne is probably the most complete fortified town in the world. Towering above the pink tile roofs of dwellings on its hillside slopes and above the green patchwork of small fertile farms in the surrounding countryside, it is encircled by not one but two stout walls. These are strengthened at intervals by some 50 massive towers. Within this fortress is a castle, a cathedral, a town of about 800 permanent residents and their small shops and cafes, and two hotels which combine the atmosphere of the Middle Ages with the comforts of the 20th century.

Within the moat (long since dry) and the Outer Wall and the tiltyard and the Inner Wall, wait the final defenses of La Cité: The castle and the cathedral, the temporal and the spiritual. The castle was an independent fortress in which the people of Carcassonne and the surrounding countryside could take refuge in time of war. The Basilica of St. Nazaire is famous for its stained glass windows. Its

Romanesque and Gothic features date back to the 11th century. Its most significant feature may be the empty tomb marked by the lion and cross of Simon de Montfort. Here, for a few years following his death in 1218, was buried the man who brought more death and suffering to the region of Languedoc, with Carcassonne at its heart, than any single conqueror in history. The intensity and bloodiness of his crusade against heretics may be divined from the reply he is reputed to have given when asked which of his opponents should be put to the sword and stake and which should be spared. "Kill them all," he said. "God will know His own."

The entrance to Carcassonne, like that ascribed to heaven, it straight and narrow. It leads to the world that existed before cannon had rendered walls obsolete, before motors and wings had diminished hilltops into easy reach, before ideas had become part of the free commerce of human life. Watching the play of light and shadow on these old towers and walls, I wondered about this era of faith and fear. And I was glad that the gate swings wide today, that the hospitality of strangers makes them friends after a few short days. I was glad I had come to Carcassonne again.

The sun shone on the ancient stones of Avignon during that afternoon in late August but an intermittent wind swept down the Rhone Valley and banished much of the sun's warmth. It also lifted the flags of 11 nations so that they rippled in all their colorful glory as each was raised on its tall standard, accompanied by the appropriate national anthem.

The occasion was the Congress of International Reserve

Officers of the NATO countries, and although France is no longer officially a member of the NATO alliance she was serving as hostess for this gathering of friends. (I, too, was not officially a member of the CIOR but was present at the invitation of friends in the American delegation.) This group represented not only different nationalities but a wide variety of professions, social backgrounds, individual personalities. Here in the courtyard of the immense Palace of the Popes they gathered in common interest and unified purpose to protect and preserve the free world.

Many who were there shared common memory of an earlier struggle to preserve that world — when it was being crushed beneath the totalitarian brutality of the Nazis. During the reception that followed these opening ceremonies and during subsequent journeys into the countryside and official events, I renewed awareness of just how much sacrifice had been demanded, and how much courage had been summoned to endure those terrible years.

The first underground hero I met was a French colonel. He was not an imposing figure — until you looked more closely at his lined and weathered face with its combination of toughness and tenderness. And when he broke his initial reserve his memories of years of trial, of living on the knife-edge of discovery, brought animation to each furrow and wrinkle. At one point, recognition of a Gestapo agent outside his office gave him only moments in which to phone friends and have the transmitter, by which he sent messages to the underground and the allies, removed from his apartment. Its discovery would have meant death. This, only one among many such narrow escapes.

There was an elegant Dane, a major whose family had been wine importers for several generations. His composure remained intact but his blue eyes grew lively with both humor and anger as he recalled and shared some of the incidents of dealing with the Germans during their occupation of his homeland. A fellow Dane, a small and lively man, recounted with emotional fervor the experience of leaving his country after the German occupation and becoming part of the Danish Resistance in London; he told of returning to Denmark with a handful of friends and blowing up a factory making batteries for the German army.

Perhaps the most moving of many similar personal accounts was that of a Dutch colonel. We began talking almost by accident near one of the long tables laden with French canapes. When he was convinced that I was genuinely interested in his experiences, not just making polite conversation, he began to speak of the harsh occupation of Holland. "Occupation of your country by an enemy is a terrible thing," he repeated several times. "It comes so gradually; each day another freedom, another friend, disappears until nothing is left." His underground activities had brought him imprisonment by the Nazis. Three times he escaped, the last time by swimming across Lake Constance into Switzerland with a bullet in his heel and in his back. Fortunately, he had a friend in Switzerland who could prove, as he said, "I am myself." He tried to make me realize what it would be like to arrive in another country without any identification during a tense time of war and turmoil. The wounds in his flesh had taken a long time to heal; the wounds to his spirit, of proving who he was in an alien world, took longer to heal. As he spoke about war and his experiences, this quiet-spoken man with firm, strong countenance momentarily had tears in his eyes. They gave his uniform a special touch of class.

These were only a few of the hundreds brought together to share information and concerns and perhaps carry useful advice back to their own governments. Many, like the handsome Italian doctor and his glamourous wife, were too young to have memories such as those of the men mentioned above. But, like the flags of their countries whipping in the wind at Avignon, they were gathered briefly to share their diversity and forge a unity in the cause of freedom.

To refute the notion that Paris is all of France and that cowboys are the exclusive property of the U.S.A., consider the Camargue.

On the southern coast of France where the two main arms of the mighty Rhone River merge into the Mediterranean there is a strange land of marshes where sea and sky and earth blend along the horizon, providing a distinctive backdrop for the humans and wildlife that flourish here. This is the Camargue. It is a land of legend and reality, of delicate beauty and harsh necessity, of people and the elements and animals part of a continuing ritual of survival.

Many years ago I enjoyed a memorable film, "White Mane," about a boy and a wild horse in the Camargue and I have wanted to see this part of France that seems in such contrast to the rest of the country.

I was happy to be a guest for a day's journey and festivities in this region. It was an unusual experience.

In the middle of the delta is the Etang de Vaccares, a large wildlife reserve noted for its flamingoes and egrets; all manner of bird and animal life finds protection around the great lagoon. In the dunes between this lagoon and the sea is the village of the Camargue, Les Saintes Maries de la Mer.

This long name derives from an even longer legend that some 40 years after the crucifixion a boat without sails or oars was set adrift from the Holy Land. It carried some of Jesus' closest companions, including three Marys and a black

219

servant named Sara. When their boat landed on this shore they began to spread the message of Christianity until finally only Sara and two companions remained here. Their tombs became shrines and each year thousands of gypsies still gather here on a pilgrimage of supplication and celebration to Sara.

Saintes Maries was simply a small, tourist seaside town the morning we stopped there and walked along the Mediterranean, watched some young campers emerge from the cocoons of bedrolls and sleeping bags, bought a croissant and a postcard.

But then we went out into the country, across wide stretches of marshland that are now being tamed by rice fields — but where there is still space for black bulls and white horses and those skilled horsemen known as *gardians.* We passed little whitewashed buildings with thatched roofs and conical tops that are characteristic of the Camargue. Ranches resembled some of those in our West — without the buildings. We arrived at a vast open meadow — with a tent shading brightly decorated tables set for the throng of visitors. Pretty girls dressed in the costumes native to Provence danced to the music of a brass band. And over smoldering fires, four beef carcasses were turning on their spits, filling the air with the aroma of smoke and meat and herbal basting.

Then the band led the way across the road to another field, where the *gardians* had assembled. Wearing hats, astride their handsome horses, they looked like our Western cowboys or South American gauchos. Slowly they rode toward a herd of midnight-black bulls milling in the distance — and swung into action, cutting a young one from the herd. At full gallop they chased it into our very midst, where unmounted helpers seized the young bull, threw it, and branded it with an iron pulled from a nearby open blaze. This was the *ferrade,* an ancient ceremony that used to be a community festivity, much like our house-raising or corn-shucking in Appalachia.

The cult of the bull remains in the Camargue, a reminder of older civilizations; here, too, the horse remains indispensable. It was exciting to glimpse the world in which they hold special significance. The poet Mistral wrote: "When the sea swells and darkens, when boats break their moorings, the stallions of Camargue whinny with happiness . . ."

There was more music and dancing during the afternoon. There was food and drink in abundance at the long tables. There was a processional march as the beef carcasses were carried in and carved. But as I looked at the weatherlined faces of the *gardians* when they joined our feast, I felt that the true reality and legend of this corner of France had merged in that moment when man and horse and bull were galloping across an open field in all their vigor and skill.

The *gardians* of the Camargue are as remote from Paris as the cowboys of Wyoming are remote from the landscape and spirit of New York. Long may their white horses "whinny with happiness."

I returned from a distant exploration and found a friend was missing.

He chose us. We did not choose him. He was smarter than we.

He arrived one morning with the mailman. After a thorough examination of our grounds he continued on his way, but reappeared with the mailman the next morning. This time he stayed.

At first we tried to ignore him. This was impossible. The brightness of his eyes and the tilt of his head when he looked at us, and the gauntness of his sides, demanded attention. After that first bowl of food and that initial exchange of greetings, we belonged to each other. He promptly established his domain.

He was not of fashionable breed or status. His genealogy was dubious. He was simply the smartest little dog we ever encountered. There was an alertness about him, an anticipation, which seemed to take in everything and everyone — and he participated in every wintertime walk in the woods, every meal on the patio, every lingering summer evening on the porch, with total enthusiasm — and taste. On the walks he heralded our advance — sniffing, leaping, circling, exploring — and then escorted us home with triumphant satisfaction. When we were at the redwood table or on a chaise lounge, he would "check in" and then post himself at a discreet distance, watchful for any morsel of meat or praise that might wander his way.

He knew schedules and people and his neighborhood with uncanny sense. Sometimes when I was up very early in the morning I would see him trotting down the street in front of our house, looking to each side, on his daily rounds of the hill where we live. At night he raised his quick bark against any intruder — two-footed or four-footed.

When he saw suitcases appear at our garage, he assumed an air of hurt disdain. He seemed to know that we would be gone for a while and that he and a caretaker would be left to look after each other. But upon each return — well, his welcome knew no bounds. And when our sons returned from school for each vacation, he struggled to speak with everything but words.

Part of his intelligence was his curiosity. He was medium-size, tan with white around the neck and on his face, and his tail — curled over his back or drooping — was like a flag signalling his mood. But wherever he was, he had to poke and prowl and participate.

He had a proud little prance of a walk, almost as if he had been trained for a circus. "He was a friend to all of us kids," our paperboy said. Above all, he had courage. He would tackle a threat twice his size. He pulled through a serious sickness that even the veterinarian could never definitely diagnose. And he hated any sort of confinement. He was quick and free and friendly.

He was standing on the grass beside the street in front of our house when a speeding car swerved and hit him.

There is a French proverb, "The best thing about a man is his dog." One of the best things about our family, for eight years, was this precocious, loyal little dog. His presence made us more aware of the uniqueness of every living creature on this earth. If his immortality is in our memory of him, he'll live for a long while.

Have you ever thought of the ways in which trees shed their leaves? Perhaps you thought that the leaves whirled down each autumn in the same style, shaken loose by the same wind. Look again.

Each species seems to have its own pattern and time schedule for "losing its hair" as the Cherokees used to describe the shedding of leaves. And each process seems to reflect something about the "character" of the tree itself.

Perhaps there is a human parallel in this subject of the varieties of ways by which life moves into new seasons.

The tree near our house which drops its leaves at the earliest opportunity is a box elder. Big and broad and never too beautiful at any time of the year, it persists in rushing the season. By mid-August it is beginning to cast off a few of its leaves and by late August, when summer seems still at its height, there are piles of small, crackling leaves under its limbs. Dry and brown they crumble underfoot with an unwelcome rustle which whispers of autumn-just-around-the-corner. The box elder seems to hurry toward hibernation. (I am not very fond of it.)

The sourwoods greet fall early, too, but with such a difference! Their leaves flush red while the rest of the woods stand green. But then they hang on a long time, making a final, graceful statement among larger, sturdier trees.

Poplars turn gradually, their yellow shades as bright as those of the first daffodils in spring. But the gold fades into brown as the broad leaves drift to the ground. Once the loosening has begun each wind seems to shake the leaves more rapidly from the limbs. The mature glory is short-lived.

Maples linger longer, some flaming scarlet and others touched with gold, some nondescript in more subdued silvery hues. And often those leaves retain their color even as they fall, creating a Persian carpet along sidewalk and on lawns. They seem intent on holding and sharing their beauty as long as possible.

Finally, there are the oaks. One great oak stands at a corner of our house. Its leaves are tenacious. They are still thick on every limb even at the time of a new year, waiting to be displaced by young buds which will push away the dry and wrinkled remainders of last summer. Lashing winds and rains, heavy ice and snows, do not defeat these persistent leaves. They will yield only to the arrival of tender new life.

They shed their foliage each year: box elder, sourwood, poplar, maple, oak. They surrender their beauty in ways as distinctive as people shed their years: Submissively or reluctantly, prematurely or tenaciously.

224

And what of the pines and balsams and cedars that stand evergreen throughout the seasons? Well, perhaps there are a few humans, too — rare, gracious, enlightened souls — who remain forever young. They are to be cultivated.

Have you ever heard anyone say Happy Labor Day? Have you ever sent a Labor Day card to anyone? Yet this is an official holiday no less than July Fourth or Thanksgiving. More than that, it is a seasonal dividing line. Labor Day marks the end of summer and the arrival of autumn. A few tomatoes may still linger on the vine. The swim suit may get wet on several other occasions. Picnics and some delayed vacationers may still be part of the landscape. But in our heart of hearts we know there is no recovery of summer's blazing glory. It is autumn and our work engages us again.

Few attitudes of Americans are more ambivalent than those we hold toward labor. We preach its joys and necessity with vigor, and practice its discipline and necessity with complaint. Recognition of the "dignity of labor" is part of our national litany, but we display secret envy of anyone who seems to have avoided experience of what we call work. Disturbing polls and surveys reveal that an astonishing number of our people are unhappy, dissatisfied in their jobs; but the accumulated wisdom of society indicates that human beings discover much of their deepest fulfillment in pursuing their work.

How do we really feel about work?

Ecclesiastes provides us contrasting thoughts. At one point we are told, "What hath man of all his labor, and of the vexation of his heart, wherein he hath labored under the sun?" And then we read, "To rejoice in his labor: This is the gift of God." Is our work a vexation or a joy? Or a mixture of the two?

The great American writer Nathaniel Hawthorne believed that "Labor is the curse of the world, and nobody can meddle with it without becoming proportionately brutified." But his contemporary and equal literary giant, Ralph Waldo Emerson, found, "When I go to my garden with a spade, and dig a bed, I feel such an exhilaration and health that I discover that I have been defrauding myself all this time in letting others do for me what I should have done with my own hands." Do we feel that work with our hands and muscles "brutifies" us or exhilarates us?

There is the viewpoint of the humorist who wrote, "I like work; it fascinates me. I can sit and look at it for hours. I love to keep it by me: The idea of getting rid of it nearly breaks my heart." And the proverb, "Work only tires a woman, but it ruins a man."

The painter Picasso poured incredible energy into work he considered more than a luxury or even an option. "Work," he said, "is a necessity for man. Man invented the alarm-clock." (I have wondered if some woman did not invent the alarm-clock, so that she could get her own and everyone else's work under way on time each morning?)

Perhaps the most important ingredient in any work is a sense of purpose. Digging a ditch may become the most important job in a city if it promotes the health of that city's citizens and avoids a possible plague. Creating a song may be a labor of immeasurable worth, reflecting and renewing aspirations of the human spirit. The noble Leonardo da Vinci whose work was both slavery and freedom, said, "God sells us all things at the price of labor." What are you buying with you labor?

Lost: Somewhere between the beginning of May and the middle of September, one summer.

Said summer is in good condition, having been used only slightly. In fact, when compared with extensive plans which were made for its use upon its first arrival, it might be said to be in practically pristine condition.

When last seen, summer was leap-frogging across hours and days and sometimes entire weeks, scampering down a trail of broken resolutions, vanished leisure, well-planned dreams. It disappeared one golden afternoon when the sun was hot and the air was still and the cicadas were loud among the leafy trees. Upon questioning, no one remembered the moment of its departure, but all could attest to its occurrence.

Reliable reports say that at last accounts summer was wearing green. There was confusion about the exact shade: Some witnesses vowed that it was an intense hue, the color of dense forest and deep seas, while others suggested that it was as pale as early willows or fern fronds in a shaded woods. There were brilliant accessories, as well; fringes of late summer lilies and lavender-blue argeratum, sunbursts of marigolds and splashes of zinnias and scarlet sage.

Summer was in good voice just before departure. There were the hums and drones and high shrill tickings of insects at lazy noontime; the busy chatter of katydids in the early dew-filled darkness. There was the sound of splashing in pools, and children playing in parks and yards, and strangers exchanging brief greetings on hiking trail or waiting room or deck of ship or a neighbor's patio. There was the music of rain after a long dry spell, and the song of birds after a soggy interval of monsoon moisture.

Lost: Somewhere between the beginning of May and the middle of September, one summer. Only slightly used. Good for at least another season. Once mislaid, forever gone.

If found, no need to return to owner. Another season has already applied for audition. In fact, the role is cast, the post is taken, the position is in order.

The vacancy, before it occurred, has been filled by impatient, fruitful autumn. "Never mind summer's abandonment," it whispers, shouts, invites. "Never mind frivolous, heady summer's leave-taking. I am here to restore empty places. I will wear colors more glorious than anything summer could boast. I will open to you the sound of my own voice. But you'd better not waste time looking for errant summer — lest I leap-frog, scamper, and vanish, too!"

Found: Somewhere between yesterday and today, one autumn!

September has always seemed to me to be a time of beginnings. Jan. 1 may be officially designated on our calendars as the beginning of a new year, but I believe that for many of us Sept. 1 is quite as much the start of a new year.

For millions of children and their parents and their teachers and all who serve the educational profession, commencement of the school year is certainly a time of beginning again. For those in the entertainment business/profession, and for those who are its patrons (which must include most of the population at one time or another), September

228

marks the opening of new seasons, new careers. For farmers and those who live on the land the season of planting and cultivating matures to the final harvest.

As I have said before in these columns, I am not very adept at "goodbys." I am more of a "hello" person.

Beginnings are filled with promise and untapped potential. The possibilities are unexplored and intriguing. Endings mark a halt, a finality beyond any recall. Readjustments must be made.

Monday morning, clean stacks of typewriter paper, new snow, a fresh linen tablecloth: All of these are "hello" things. They await the miracle of use, the first mark or step or unexpected event.

Cabooses, ashes, "Auld Lang Syne," sunsets, and final scores: These are "goodby" things. They signify the last of the train hurtling by, the dying of the fire, the waning of years or days, or the big game.

There are "appetizer" people and "dessert" people. Those who savor the salt and tang and variety of hors d'oeuvres are often too stuffed to enjoy the riches of dessert. And those who await the delights of the sweets may never discover the delectability of the appetizer.

Robert Browning wrote about "the last of life for which the first was made." But if it would be all the same to him, I'd trade back again for the first of life and start making all over again. It's not the youthfulness as such that is so enticing – it is the job of beginning, of anticipation.

Goodbys comes in all styles and sizes.

Goodbys may relieve your mind or break your heart. Either way, it is likely that you will have to stifle the emotion and make it seem an ordinary event, totally expected and accepted.

But the best goodbys are forerunners of hellos that may come later. I have never told a member of my family or a friend goodby that I did not think about the next time we would meet. There are certain people whose goodbys fill me with expectancy, for I know that the next time we meet they will have a fund of stories, experiences, opinions, to share with me.

In such cases perhaps it is best to remember the German proverb, "Beginning and end shake hands with each other."

That would seem to indicate that there is no such thing as a goodby or hello person. If we start with enthusiasm and hope, that is what we shall meet in the end. Perhaps in the future I should simply take leave (of people or places or experiences) by saying "Hello!" Thus end and beginning are one.

A month in England and Scotland renews acquaintance with the roots of many Appalachian people and serves as reminder of many half-forgotten experiences. For instance, it was a joy to rediscover the glory of the English garden.

In the cities, in villages, and scattered across the countryside, there are those roses — pure pink and scarlet and dark maroon, yellow as gold, white as unblemished snow — flourishing in late September and early October as if it were our midsummer. Tall as a man's shoulder, such specimens must be the despair of American rose growers who visit the British Isles. And when a friend I visited told me that she never sprayed or dusted her roses, I was glad that I had long since resigned as a competitor in this particular realm of gardening. Climate, soil, perhaps even the English character, must combine to create such perfect conditions for production of the queen of flowers.

But just as impressive to me is the creaton of private and public gardens with ordinary, familiar flowers — even the varieties that I can coax into bloom. During leisurely walks along city streets or on longer ventures through the country-side, there is constant surprise and pleasure in discovering patterns of color, texture, arrangement that makes the ordinary seem extraordinarily beautiful.

Marigolds, petunias, argeratum, dahlias, sweet alyssum, lobelia, old-fashioned golden glows and large bushes of fus-chias: These are a few of the "oldies" that the TLC (tender loving care) of gardening hands turned into "goodies." Even the flowers that we dismiss as weeds — wild blue asters and goldenrod — are often featured in such manner that they be-come stars instead of outcasts.

In many of the squares before modest cottages or small "row" houses, vegetables are incorporated into these patches of flowering beauty — and in a way that makes them seem pretty, too. Broccoli and lettuce, gracefully climbing beans, onions and beets: All assume a special dignity when treated as special guests and not mere necessities. These gardens, integrating feasts for the spirit and for the stomach, stand as testimonials to the truth that humans do not live by either bread or beauty alone.

Of course, there are an incredible number of famous gardens that visitors to any part of England may discover. Northwest of London, in the lovely Cotswold hills of Gloucestershire, are gardens that have been called the most beautiful of the 20th century. They are Hidcote Manor Gardens, the creation of an American Army officer. In 1907 Maj. Lawrence Johnston began to transform a high, rather wind-swept, unkempt site, which boasted one fine cedar and two groups of beech trees, into a botanical paradise. And this is the distinction of Hidcote: It is a series of small gar-

231

dens, each set off by luxuriant hedges and all linked by meandering green walks, balancing the spaciousness of 10 acres of rare and commonplace plants with the privacy of enclosed spaces featuring one particular color or species of plants. In one compartment, for instance, all the flowers and shrubs are red in blossomor leaf. In one segment, moisture-loving ferns thrive; in another, plants that require dry conditions flourish. All of the contrast is bound together by green vistas and deep-piled carpets of lawns.

Such showplaces as Hidcote Manor are delightful. But the real soul of the English gardener remains in those little home plots, cherished, nurtured.

At the end of a recent journey to become reacquainted with the British Isles, I had an experience that helped me become reacquainted with myself.

I went to the morning services at St. Giles Cathedral in Edinburgh. Scottish skies had turned blue and clear following a night of fog and rain, and the walk from the "New City" (merely two centuries old) to the Old Town (exact age unknown) was as refreshing as the crisp breeze. The forbidding battlements of the ancient castle, where memories of Mary, Queen of Scots, still linger, loomed like an almost human presence against the horizon. There is about that dark fortification, with its walls and towers and barriers, a sense of the tragedy of history. Hatred, struggle for power, death by warfare and treachery and disease and despair, are part of that great, grim structure and its message.

Not far from the castle, along the Royal Mile that leads to Holyrood House, the royal palace at the other end of the

232

city, stands St. Giles. Its grey stones, too, are dark and heavy — but within, its soaring vaulted interior lifts the eyes and mind upward. The Gothic architectural purpose of carrying human attention away from self and into a higher realm is achieved once more.

"For over a thousand years this place has known Christian worship," a brochure of welcome says. And visitors are assured that St. Giles, "as Edinburgh's city church, is known and loved by people of many churches and of none. The worship and administration have followed the changing stages of the Church of Scotland — Roman, Episcopalian, and currently Presbyterian." A thousand years is a substantial time in which to put down roots! A Presbyterian cathedral! A visitor had many thoughts in this place.

An invitation included in the welcome kindled further thought: "It is our hope that you will find here a true sense of the mystery and hope of the Christian Gospel, and that you will be able to enter into a heritage of disturbing faith and courageous discipleship in the cause of life and growth and peace."

First it was startling, and then it was challenging, and finally it was invigorating to see faith referred to as "disturbing." And what more could we include in a sense of purpose than life, growth, peace?

Morning sunlight illuminated the rich stained glass of St. Giles' windows and suffused the grey interior with a warm radiance. The scarlet robes of the choir contrasted with the pewter grey of columns and walls and fan-shaped arching ceiling.

The young visiting minister spoke simply and eloquently on sorrow. "Jesus wept" was his text, but the raising of Lazarus was his message.

He spoke of the selfishness that is part of much of our sorrow. His words touched my mind like the sun's ray touched one of the tattered banners of an old chiefdom just over my head. Grief that can seize us at an unexpected moment, distract us and diminish us: How often has mine been selfish only!

As I came out of St. Giles and walked across the city, the old castle seemed slightly less solitary and awesome. Its closed towers were answered by St. Giles' open doors. Sunday had been a rewarding day of rediscovering part of Edinburgh and myself.

Whatever happened to breakfast?

Somewhere between yesterday and today, breakfast was lost, strayed or stolen.

Lost, perhaps, to the urgencies of schedules and commuter trains and car pools. Strayed into other forms — such as brunch and coffees. Stolen by diets and coffee breaks at the office and late night TV snacks.

But there was a time when breakfast was a whole meal, a gathering around the family table. An occasion. There were glasses of juice and bowls of fruit — ranging from fresh strawberries in the spring to hot applesauce in the summer and autumn. Bacon was crisp and crumbly and had the smoky taste of solid reality; sausage was lean and flavorsome and truly "country;" ham was succulent and yielded a red-eye juice that lent distinction to any other food it touched — eggs or bread or grits.

There were eggs — large, brown, fresh, fresh, fresh. They stood firm in frying pan or poacher, and blended to a golden softness when scrambled over a low heat.

And the bread! Biscuits light and flaky, ready to soak

234

butter and blackberry jam or grape jelly or orange marmalade to a melted sweetness. Rolls so tempting in their aroma that the reality of their luscious lightness seemed almost an anticlimax to the anticipation. Or toast, browned to an even amber in the oven so that butter could melt in with just the right flavor and proportion — not too much for sogginess, not too little for dryness.

Sometimes there were hot cakes, thin and steaming, or waffles, crisply golden to carry the unique satisfaction of pure maple syrup with every coveted morsel.

Breakfast means wildly different things in different places. On a wheat farm in Kansas it still means fuel to stoke a human engine for along day's physical pull. In a New York office it may mean coffee and a cigarette during the first coffee break. To a back-packer in the wilderness it can mean fresh trout cooked over an open fire.

In most European hotels, the continental breakfast of rolls and coffee, tea or chocolate may be delectable or disappointing, depending on the hard rolls or croissants accompanying the inevitable marmalade or jam.

In Norway, I remember an early morning repast in the fjord country that included pickled herring, smoked salmon, and several other varieties of fish, Danish ham and bacon, eggs in a number of styles, sour cream, and long loaves of flavorsome, richly textured bread. In the early morning freshness of wind off the still waters of the fjord, surrounded by the pinnacles of towering, mist-covered mountains, the heavily laden table of the long dining room seemed entirely appropriate and appetizing.

Sometimes when I see the rows of cereal boxes on the supermarket shelves, I remember that morning in Norway. And accounts I have read and heard of breakfasts of yesteryear here in our own region. Fried chicken and generous ladles of gravy, freshly picked corn creamed to a savory richness, eaten with hot biscuits, sourwood honey, and scalding coffee, or ice cold milk. Porridge cooked in a double boiler the night before, with the nutty taste of the oats or wheat preserved in all its fullness. And sometimes — think of it! — hot doughnuts, or a wedge of apple pie.

No diet-watcher's nibbles were these. Calories and cholesterol counts must have been astronomical. But what a way to go. And what a way to begin a day. Perhaps that was part of the difference between yesterday and today. Our ancestors' strenuous physical labors burned up the fuel provided by such hearty food. Our work today requires, in large part, a different kind of energy.

Where is the menu that will provide our mind power the hearty and delectable menu once demanded by our muscle power? Then, perhaps, we will not have to reach for a bottle of pills and wonder, whatever happened to breakfast?

The young mountain man told me of his prize as matter-of-factly as early hunters must have told of bagging passenger pigeons, as triumphant seamen must have told of harpooning great whales.

"We were on our way home from town one Saturday afternoon. You see, I work in a plant that's a pretty far piece from our home way back here on the mountain and I have to leave before daylight and get back just about dark five days a week, so there's no chance for us to go to the grocery store or anything except on a Saturday.

"Well, we had the two young'uns in the back of our '69 Chevy and we were heading home that Saturday afternoon and just before we come into that big curve on the new

236

highway down there alongside the national forest my wife let out a scream worse than an old she-pant'er. I was just hitting the brakes when she yelled, 'I saw it! Laying right there in the woods in plain sight. I saw it!'

"I didn't bother with the brakes then, just went on around the curve while I asked her what she saw back in the woods that would make her yell like that and she said, 'It was a deer — a white deer! Laying there in an open place among the big old trees with the sun flecking down on it through the limbs and leaves. A plumb white deer.'

"Now I'd heard tell of such a creature. I understand the Cherokee Indians used to have a regular hymn or chant or whatever you call it to the spirit of the white deer. But till that afternoon I reckon I'd thought of it all more as a big tale than anything else. But when my wife hollered out that way and told me about seeing — what is it they call it? an albino deer — right then I said to myself, 'This is it. Here's something way out of the common run, something strange.'

"So I told her and the young'uns — they were all excited and jumping around on the back seat — to quieten down and I drove on home as fast as I could. I unloaded the family. I carried in the groceries. Then I went in the back room and got my rifle.

"I drove back up the highway till I come to the open place in the woods beyond the big curve. I slowed and I stretched my eyes a-looking. Then all at once I saw it. The white deer was still laying down. But its head was high, alert, not a muscle moving.

"I understood why my wife had cried out the way she did. That whiteness amongst all the green with the evening sun dappling down on it, and the stillness everywhere, it gave off a queer sort of feeling.

"A little farther on, along the shoulder of the highway, I parked my car. When I killed the motor I tell you everything was really quiet. There didn't seem to be the usual traffic along that way just then and there wasn't even any wind stirring in the mountains. I could fairly hear myself breathing. I reached to the back seat and picked up my rifle and made sure for the second time that it was loaded.

"There wasn't any trick a-tall to taking that deer. When I eased through the woods to where I could take aim it was laying just like I'd seen it. I'd say it was still as a statue — but that would be exactly wrong because that deer was alive. The eyes. The ears. Even that satin-white skin seemed like it was breathing. If I'd studied that creature half a minute longer I'm doubtful I could have squeezed the trigger.

"My shot was a good direct hit. The deer didn't hardly get afoot and running before it fell. The blood sure soaked red against that white skin.

"I felt downright queer when I come up to that carcass and stood there along with a prize no man I actually knowed had ever seen before. It was like looking at a ghost spirit. Or something — you know, pure.

"It dressed out nice. We gave a lot of the meat to folks around here. The hide is in yonder right now — in that big old freezer. I don't know exactly what to do with it. But there must be something real special to do with a white deer hide."

When goldenrod and wild blue asters fringe the roadsides, when squirrels bustle through the hickory and oak trees harvesting their winter's store, when dust at midday is settled by a white crust of frost each night, is an appropriate season for family gatherings.

October's ripeness stirs nostalgia. Autumn's nip is reminder of the future. Between the memory of yesterday and the anticipation of tomorrow — today is a good time to renew the bonds with those we call "family."

Nowhere in the country are those bonds stronger than in the region where we live. At a time when the definition of family has come to mean, for many people, only a father and mother and children, we still include grandparents and uncles and second cousins once removed among our active kinships.

And when one of those distinctive occasions called a "family reunion" occurs, everyone renews his sense of just how each relationship came about. When I was a child I remember going to one of these events where my great-grandfather sat in patriarchal dignity on an October afternoon to receive the tribute of youngsters only 60 or 70 years old.

He had served in the Civil War; through him I realized that history was people — and that it did not die but lived on in the consequences flowing from each event, every encounter. From him I also learned that old age did not have to be melancholy, that it could enjoy its privileges — and share a twinkle in the eye.

Throughout our region allegiance to family persists. Virginian Clifford Dowdey has described his state's strong feeling: "The center of Virginia's parochial society has always been the family — indeed, the state is something of a family. The basis is not, as is commonly thought 'ancestor worship,' though certainly there are awesome bores on the subject . . . The family is simply the thing of value, as is wealth in a money society."

Of Kentucky, a native has written: "When his ancestors crossed the Appalachians, the family was the core of community life and the Kentuckian has never lost sight of the importance of his family attachment."

And the editor of one of Charleston's major newspapers told us of West Virginia: "Consider the fact that from late June through each October our newspaper — and I'll lay wagers on this — prints more notices of family reunions than any other paper in the country. One family I know in an adjoining county has thousands who come to their reunion each year. Fifty thousand were reported by the wire services one year! It's like a gathering of the clans."

Well, 50,000 relatives might be a little excessive — even if each one brought his own lunch. And with my poor memory for names I can only imagine my constant embarrassment when confronted with that challenge. But for a moment, here in October, there is something nourishing in remembrance of those ties — to heroes and scoundrels, "successes" and "failures" — who make up all the variety and humanity of each person's family.

Pride goeth before a fall. So I have been told by people who have expertise in such matters. Alas, I discover that they are probably correct.

One of the achievements (an humble thing, I admit, but mine own) in which I have taken some pride during recent seasons has been my conquest of a formidable enemy. A silent, resilient, determined enemy — the worst kind of opponent.

At first I did not perceive this foe in all its greed, devastation and downright impudence. I thought of it as friend and confederate in good causes, an attractive and bountiful colleague seeking a better life for us both.

The truth dawned gradually, then with mounting certainty. Once I began to comprehend the voracious appetite and invincible vitality of my enemy, I grew more and more dismayed. Any my enemy grew more and more.

Finally it became apparent: One of us had to go! The kudzu and I could not share the same homeplace. These few acres were not sufficient to hold both the kudzu roots and mine. Drawing on Clausewitz, Napoleon, memory of the class bully in my fifth grade, and other military strategists, I determined that my course must be that of an offensive. (After all, the kudzu had become thoroughly offensive to me, why shouldn't I return the compliment?)

As I sought allies in my struggle, I discovered the strength of my enemy. When I mentioned "kudzu," strong men flinched and turned the subject to other matters. Keepers of gardening shops and hardware stores — standing in the midst of dozens of steel tools and acres of bottles and boxes of poisons — shook their heads and regarded me with expressions of mingled astonishment and pity. At my foolhardy insistence (we military strategists do not like to be thrown off our plan), one clerk did sell me some spray material. "It's supposed to make the kudzu grow itself to death," he said. But there was no triumph in his tone.

There was no triumph in the spray either. It made kudzu grow itself to death the way raw beef makes a lion grow itself to death. Nourishment was all that I succeeded in achieving with that attack.

Friends and neighbors warned me of the defeat that would conclude my struggle. As I drove across the South I saw miles, acres, jungles of land and forest that were completely devoured by my enemy. That's the trouble with kudzu: It doesn't deprive you of its blessings, it overwhelms you with them. It embraces everything to death. The bluff across the street from my home, leading down to the river, was being devoured. A small orchard of chestnut trees was

241

choked to death. Redbud and dogwood had long since disappeared. In three or four seasons, the world we had planned — or preserved, in the case of the big oaks, maples, and woods on the steep part of the bluff — was vanishing. Tough, tangled leaves and tendrils of kudzu gobbled up new areas every day of the growing season. I had visions of awaking some morning to find that kudzu had crossed the street and was reaching into my bedroom window to bury me under its tangled benevolence.

One last plan of attack remained. I approached a local road-builder and asked him if he had a machine stout enough and a driver foolhardy enough to tackle my kudzued bluff. He did and they did. For two days that giant machine pushed trees into a ravine, shoved out tangled bushes, even disturbed the kudzu. At last, that ravenous vine was uprooted.

Those who had been skeptical seemed pleased by my onslaught against my opponent. I planted grass and nurtured the land back to order and looked at the tall trees gracing, unmolested, the remainder of the steep hillside. I was proud in my small victory.

Then came the fall. Articles begain to appear, and acquaintances (I cannot call them friends) began to show me the articles, describing the immense virtues of kudzu. It "stabilizes road banks" and "rejuvenates nitrogen-deficient soil." And who can doubt that the Japanese and Chinese make baskets, paper, cloth and flour from these vines? Here in my own front yard I had a stabilizer and rejuvenator that could have improved several million desert acres — if anyone could have found the earth beneath the vines. Here in my own doorway I had the raw material for hundreds of issues of "True Confessions" and tons of Kleenex, flour enough to make a pattycake for every other Chinese child — if someone had set up a factory or mill. Was my adversary really my ally, providing me the possibility of a fortune I had

242

pushed down the drain?

My pride is shaken. Then I read that "an estimated 1 million acres or more of Southern farm, forest, and pasture land are now covered by kudzu." I settle back to enjoy my spacious trees and green grass; let someone else make a fortune in baskets. I'm glad that there is now only 999,998 acres "covered by kudzu" in the South.

Greece is not the place most recently explored but it is the place most often remembered. Its beauty cannot be captured on these pages but nuggets of wisdom can be scattered through my explorations like segments of the shattered columns which lie strewn over the grass in the tawny light of Olympia.

There is a summons to courage in the admonition of the playwright Aeschylus: "Take heart. Suffering, when it climbs highest, lasts but a little time."

And call to another kind of courage in the words of playwright Euripides: "A slave is he who cannot speak his thought."

A book, a bedspread and a ring.

Things, we sometimes say, are not to be too much cherished. Ideas, wisdom, freedom from possessions: these are treasures to be pursued. But each of these possessions — book, bedspread, and ring — carries special meaning. Each relates to experiences of Greece.

The book.

It does not compete for attention. Its serviceable dark green cover bears the simple identification, *Ten Greek Plays*. Oxford. Among brightly jacketed, cleverly titled, current companions it sits on the bookshelf the way a legendary Boston matron in her good tweeds and genuine jewels rests among flashy newcomers who follow transient fads and fashions. Its quiet exterior enfolds the breadth and depth of human experience.

When I arrived at Northwestern University, years ago, to study drama — and English and history and a few other minors — I was unacquainted with our Greek heritage. A course in the history of the theater introduced me to Sophocles, Aeschylus, Euripides, Aristophanes. The greatest of their plays were collected in a volume I checked out of the library. But the copy I really coveted was in an Evanston bookstore. Compact, fresh, pristine, 475 pages of intrigue, terror, pride, passion, satire, human frailty, and nobility. My limited budget didn't permit purchase of the book. I visited it from time to time. Then one day a classmate casually presented me with a gift. I owned *Ten Greek Plays!*

I owned Antigone's plea: "Not in your hates, but in your loves, I'd share."

I owned Electra's despair: "I cried for dancing of old, I cried in my heart for love."

And I owned Agamemnon's warning: "I reckon no man blest ere to the utmost goal his race be run;" so close akin to the wisdom of Oedipus:" . . . and no man's life account as gain

Ere the full tale be finished and the darkness find him without pain."

All the years to follow were needed, of course, to come into true possession of that volume. And many years passed

244

before I made a pilgrimage to the origins of this heritage, half afraid that the place itself would prove a disappointment, that expectations were too high. I need not have worried. Greece — the mainland and the endlessly varied islands — lived up to and beyond all hopes.

To hold *Ten Greek Plays* in my hand and turn its pages is to recapture an identification with place — harsh and beautiful, mountainous, washed by sea and sun — which was and is Greece.

The bedspread.

It is white and a refreshing yellow the shade of Corfu's lemons, made of wool sheared, carded, spun, dyed, and woven by hands of Greek hill women, and it will not wear out in two lifetimes. Its weight alone could have put us over the allowed quota if airline officials had been picky about our luggage as we came home. Perhaps some oracle informed them about the place where we found this lovely weaving.

We came upon the little girl and her grandmother in the village of Arakhova. Arakhova itself is not usually a destination. It perches on well-watered terraces along the sides of Mt. Parnassus where the road to Delphi winds steeply upward. Travelers on the way to Delphi pause to enjoy Arakhova's setting of scenic grandeur and the bright flowers, small fruits and vegetables that flourish on the terraces. Every patch of available soil is put to use. Existence here does not come without effort. There are many displays of handicrafts for sale.

On Mt. Parnassus in Arakhova I wandered into a home that was also a shop. Its small, intense proprietor reminded me of girls I have known in Southern Appalachia: at once shy and eager, friendly but suspicious from past wounds to pride inflicted by thoughtless visitors. Her dark eyes watched me closely.

I looked at embroidery work displayed on a table but my

245

real interest was in the woven goods on shelves along the sides of the room. We talked — not in my non-existent Greek but in her quite respectable English, she the more literate one. Her young face, already weathered by wind and sun, grew animated as she unfolded various items, described colors and patterns. I inquired about prices, especially on the large yellow and white spread. She ran into an adjoining room.

An older, unsteady voice became audible. There was animated conversation, truly all Greek to me. Then, in a moment of silence, I saw a face peer around an edge of the door. All was black — shawl, dress, stockings, shoes — except for the face as lined and rough as the land outside her window. The face disappeared and the girl returned.

"I have said to my grandmother that you chose this one," she patted my bedspread and her eyes shone. "She is old and you have made her very happy."

After that there was no turning back. I had bought a bedspread whether or not I meant to. Of course I meant to. I look at it now and see more than good material and a pattern and colors I like. I see Arakhova set in splendid mountain scenery on the road to Delphi and a little girl-woman akin to all those around the world who shoulder early in life responsibilities and satisfactions of being part of a family.

The ring.

My ring is a heavy grape leaf design in gold set with three amethysts. It is of modest value to anyone but me.

The friends we visited in Athens had lived previously on the hills which look out over the city and the Acropolis. Later they redecorated an old house in the Plaka quarter, that jumble of streets, antiquities, shops, markets, tavernas, the oldest part of Athens, in the shadow of the Acropolis, site of the ancient Agora, where the verve, glory, sounds, sights, smells, and alertness of Athens seem to be represented in one bubbling cauldron. To walk from the tumult of the Plaka up the Acropolis to the serenity of the Parthenon and its attendant Erechtheion, Theater of Dionysos, and ruins of other temples and tombs, is to move quickly from a surging present to a noble (and crumbling) past — and to appreciate at both levels that characteristic Greek ingredient I can only identify as "energy."

Situated in the heart of the city, we discovered the life of Athens in a special way. Early morning walks accumulated fresh supplies of bread just lifted from the oven, assorted fruits, especially plump grapes bursting with juice, to be eaten at leisurely breakfast on the sun-dappled patio.

Any hour of day or night was interesting in the Plaka. And beyond its varied, crowded shops was Syntagma Square, nerve center of modern Athens. Here were the government buildings, hotels, cafes — one of which provided an especially pleasant evening after enjoying the opera with a Greek musician and his wife. And along nearby streets leading from the Square were shops, several glorious shops whose keepers made commerce at best, an art, and at the least a social exchange.

In one such establishment I spied my ring. Buying jewelry was not part of my Greek agenda or budget. I looked, sighed, and departed. A few days later another stroll took me past (and into) the same shop. The quick fox of a jeweler jumped to his showcase. I looked, tried on the ring, made an offer (which was rejected), sighed, and departed. A few weeks later, the day before we were to leave Athens, by some odd chance I found myself at the jewelry shop again. The ring was still there. I looked, tried on again, sighed, and the shopkeeper made an offer. I counted out the last drachmas in my purse. The ring was mine.

With it came a host of memories which have accompanied me through several years, many places, and some uncharted

247

explorations.

A book, a bedspread, and a ring. Things of value, not to store in a safety deposit box but to serve as mementoes in summoning courage to negotiate daily odysseys.

They help me respond to ancient Sophocles inquiry, as relevant today as in those long centuries past:

"When youth has gone,
Taking with it vain follies,
Who can ever free himself,
Bowed beneath a thousand memories?"

I am not surprised that Greece was the subject of the world's first tourist guide. In the Second Century A.D. the Greek-speaking Pausanias yielded to an urge which has afflicted many visitors to Greece: the effort to capture in words the honey-colored light that bathes the noble Parthenon, the varied landscape extending from the white columns of Poseidon's Temple on the steep headland of Cape Sounion, where Homer's blue "waves with their countless smiles" once carried a mighty Persian fleet toward its destruction at Salamis, to the barren, rugged heights of Mt. Parnassus looking down the silvery-grey groves of olive trees on the plain of Itea to the distant sparkling Gulf of Corinth.

Between and beyond these extremes of restless sea and stoic mountains are countless images of geography, art, myth, and daily life which have proved as troublesome to interpret as the riddle of the Sphinx. Such a challenge includes:

• The architectural sweep and acoustical wonder of the theater at Epidaurus where Greeks once thronged to share the drama of life's nobility and absurdity.

• The massive beehive Tomb of Agamemnon in the darkly legendary setting of Mycenae with its echoes of the doomed House of Atreus, a somber contrast to the murdered king's burnished gold mask in the Athens Archaeological Museum.

• The groves of green and peaceful Olympia with fragrance of wild thyme; the stark monasteries of the Meteora upthrust toward heaven; the red-tiled roofs and narrow streets of pleasant Nauplia.

• The rich, wide plain of Thessaly where cotton bolls swell white and heavy and I half expected to hear someone in the fields singing, "Pick that cotton, tote that bale . . . "

• Levadhia, at the mouth of a gorge where waters from one stream formed the ancient Spring of Memory and from another stream created the Spring of Forgetfulness. Which would you choose to drink from?

• Evening approaching across the fertile plain, unites the world's farms and villages in kindred rhythms. Gray's *Elegy Written In A Country Churchyard* (does anyone read it today?) as true in today's Thessaly as in yesterday's England. Carts, homeward bound, many driven by women, resemble those in Ireland and along some of the roads in northern China. Men clustered around a tractor discuss mechanical mysteries as eagerly as any "shade-tree mechanics" in Appalachia.

• In October in Greece pyracantha flames like a torch in gardens large and small, along terraces and village streets, in unexpected corners. And there is the full bloom of heavy-headed dahlias, begonias, lacy cosmos, elegant roses, in contrast to the olive groves, dark evergreens, and stony harshness of the mountains.

• Strolling through the Plaka, looking up to the Acropolis, past and present merge. The cool, harmonious beauty of

249

the classical past appeals to head, to intellect, while the body is surrounded by present, earthy smells of hot chestnuts and ripe fruits from vendors' carts, smells of rubber and leather, woolens and cottons, old copper and books. Caught between the lofty and the mundane I remember an observation of the English writer, Landor: "The Greeks soar but keep their feet on the ground." Does the old man hanging bird cages beside his crowded stall ever look up to the majestic Parthenon — and wonder? Does the old woman arranging her crocheted shawls for display sometimes glance up to the Temple of Athena Nike — and reflect? Does the boy fashioning used rubber tires into buckets shaped like coal scuttles ever catch sight of the Erechtheion — and aspire?

• Comparing the quiet fields where the war-like Sparta once flourished and the beauty that still embellishes its rival Athens, the evidence is clear that military might is transient, art endures. The spoils of war vanish, creations of the imagination survive. Who visits Sparta today or can name its heroes? Millions make the pilgrimage to Athens. The victories of Sparta have been defeated by time. The art of Athens has grown fresher, more significant, with age.

Olympia is a site which offers striking contrast to much of Greece. Watered by the Alpheios River, it is a lush green landscape where pines and poplars, evergreen oaks and the ever-present olive trees cast deep shadows over the massive remains of temples and treasuries, the grass-covered stadium and the gymnasium. It was late afternoon and early evening as we wandered over this impressive sanctuary, serene in its natural simplicity, awesome in the size and magnificence of its man-made ruins. Smell of the pines was pungent. The silence seemed that of all the centuries that had intervened between that first Olympiad and our present day. The moment was good, ripe with a sense of identification, of response.

The original Olympics were not only games, of course, but religious festivals as well. The immense temple of Zeus, dominated by its gold and ivory statue of Zeus, and the earlier temple to Hera, and the dwellings for priests who attended the games, and the treasuries which were filled with the artistic riches sent by various cities, attest to the religious nature of these celebrations. Olympia was never a city; it was a sacred precinct, a sanctuary. The games held here involved all of Greece.

Growth in the variety of contests was recorded by Pausanias, who wrote in the latter half of the second century A.D. about the rise of the Olympic Games: "At the point at which the unbroken tradition of the Olympiads begins, there were at first prizes for the foot-race . . . Afterwards, in the fourteenth Olympiad, the double foot-race was added . . . In the eighteenth Olympiad they remembered the pentathlum and the wrestling . . . In the twenty-third Olympiad they restored the prizes for boxing . . . In the twenty-fifth they admitted the race of full-grown horses (in four-horse chariots)." In the year 69 A.D. the Emperor Nero decided to come from Rome and participate himself. Although he was thrown from the ten-horse chariot he had chosen to drive, he was declared the victor. It was a low moment in Olympic history.

Throughout the entire history of the Games, however, it was the fleet runner who received the highest honor. As the winner of the foot race stood on the final day before the altar of Zeus and received the olive wreath upon his head, he heard the heralds call his name, the name of his father, and the name of his city. His glory was that of his family and his native city as well.

To beautiful Olympia came the crowds, as one writer has said, perhaps 50,000 people, the Greeks' white robes and in late years the colorful finery of foreign potentates contrasting with the tanned nude bodies of the athletes. Women could not participate or even attend the Games. (It may have taken a few thousand years, but at least we have made progress in respect to that bias.)

Significant today is the fact that during each Olympiad of ancient times, "contestants and spectators traveled under a sacred truce that was respected even by the bitterest enemies." Even when Persia was threatening to overrun Greece, and when the mighty city-states of Athens and Sparta were fighting the bloody Peloponnesian War, the Games were held under the Olympic Truce. The spirit of that truce has been described: "During the week of the celebrations the competitors, while not forgetting that they were Athenians, Spartans, Milesians, Syracusans, or whatever, remembered that they were Greeks, and they regarded an Olympic victory as the highest possible honor. The simple reward of a crown of wild olive not only immortalized the victor and his family, but redounded to the glory of his native city." Would that we could recapture this spirit in our own troubled world.

And: The Olympic festival offered fare for the whole person — mind and spirit as well as body. Although it featured athletic prowess, the presence of historians, orators and philosophers provided an opportunity for them to read their works aloud to the assembled throngs. At the Olympic Games Herodotus read extracts from his history. Poetry and musical contests were sometimes honored. Imagine such variety, such interweaving of human gifts and prowess, being part of 20th Century Olympiads.

252

Across the centuries the surge and glory, the sweetness of triumph and the gall of defeat, the honor for excellence won through discipline of mind and muscle, bind participants today with those at Olympia in Greece in a distant yesterday.

Balancing our needs as distinctive individuals and as social creatures is sometimes difficult and always challenging. Most of us achieve a sort of shifting middle ground where we mingle and share with our fellow humans and then seek out oases of isolation where we can rediscover and renew ourselves.

There are a few people throughout history who have found fulfillment in the extremes, of course: Mingling to the maximum with crowds and congregations — or withdrawing into lonely solitude. In central Greece there is an awesome place, called the Meteora, where men once abandoned the turbulent world of human affairs to strive for closer communion with a spiritual reality. They chose a dramatic site for their retreat.

The Meteora is a great cluster of rock domes, pillars, pinnacles thrusting up from a level and fertile plain to heights of 1800 feet above sea level. Because of their expanse and height, they are difficult to capture in a single picture; the impact of a first glimpse of them is impossible to distill into words. In a land rich in legend it has been noted that "the intimidating size of these rocks and their strange isolated shapes suggest some savage confrontation of old earth-born giants, here turned to stone."

It is interesting that there is no Greek myth about the genesis of these rocks. Human imagination seems unnecessary where nature's originality has been so profound. In the

253

United States the incredible scenic wonder created by time and a river is the Grand Canyon. In Greece it is the Meteora.

The name derives from the root word for meteor and meteorite "between heaven and earth," "things up in the air." Anyone who follows the narrow, twisting roads that thread their way among and up these vertical monoliths will feel between heaven and earth, hoping not to arrive at the one or leave the other too soon!

Yet here, six centuries ago, hermits weary of the battles between Serbian emperors and Byzantium and monks dedicated to a search for purity and contemplation, made this their final haven. Where only eagles and ravens had nested, they built 24 monasteries, precariously perched atop various of the forbidding granite pillars. Endowed by royal patrons, some of the monasteries eventually became treasuries of fine carvings, icons, frescoes, manuscripts. Women were not allowed even for brief visits. Accessible only by ladders, or by nets hoisted up by a windlass, these utterly lonely sites eventually fell into disrepair. Today only five remain. Lashing wind and snow have swept away most of the vestiges of the other structures.

When we visited here in late October, it was easy to believe the story that the first builder of a monastery rode up on an eagle. One of the sites is now a nunnery, reached after a dizzy ride up the precipitous road across a bridge spanning a chasm some thousand feet deep.

How harsh and elemental the life within the stone walls seemed, and the few nuns who live there were determined not to be seen by prying visitors.

We caught only glimpses of disappearing black skirts. Among the dark rocks, whitewashed walls, rough sheets drying on a line, the only color was in the flowers growing in pots, pails, pans — much as in our Southern mountains: Begonias, fuchsia, marigolds. At another monastery, more

254

than 100 steps carved into the wall of rock led up to the entrance. But that unnerving climb was still better than the string bag that was used until 1932 — swinging the crouching visitor out over the plunging valley while he or she was gradually being hauled up with the windlass hoist. When we looked at the old apparatus with its worn wooden spokes and frazzled rope, its bearded keeper told us a familiar tale: The abbot was asked by nervous strangers, "When do you change the rope?" and he replied, "When it breaks."

As we retreated from the Meteora, the monasteries shrank into mere playthings, dwarfed by the monoliths that rise like immense humps of whales or the backs of dolphins arching suddenly out of their surrounding habitat of land instead of the sea — naked, smooth, dark grey shading to black, shiny, impenetrable. We left them to the birds circling their dizzy heights and depths — and to the memories of those who once sought life by retreating from life here in this strange landscape.

The streets in the residential area of Athens where we were visiting did not churn with their customary Greek traffic and turmoil on Sunday afternoon. Cars moved at a more leisurely pace, couples strolled casually between sleek new apartment buildings and ancient ruins presently in process of excavation. A mellow glow replaced the usual brilliant light that suffuses the Greek Isles, bathing the churches of today's Orthodox religion and yesterday's Byzantine glory with a golden patina. The Acropolis itself, with its cluster of architectural treasures, seemed less distant in its lofty splendor and merged with the city at its feet.

255

Such an afternoon called for a walk, and we found a beckoning site nearby. Just across the street from the marble steps and doorway that led into our friends' residence was the Kerameikos Cemetery. Who would have believed that a cemetery could put us very much in touch with life — the life of another people in an ancient time, and yet like ourselves in small familiar ways?

The Kerameikos Cemetery lay outside the largest of the city gates of Athens, the Dipylon. This double gate, built after one of the Greek victories over the Persians, was part of the city wall constructed 479 years Before Christ. The cemetery extended alongside two principal roads and contained public tombs of men who were especially distinguished or who had fallen in war. Along other roads and paths were tombs which have yielded the museum at the cemetery and the National Museum in another part of Athens interesting marble monuments, massive vases, grave reliefs and paintings, and many a stele (a slab or pillar of stone, sometimes sculptured or painted) depicting some aspect of the life or character of the deceased.

As we walked among these mementoes scattered thickly over the terrace-like landscape, we began to feel a sense of kinship with the people who had walked — and run, skipped, limped, danced, plodded — here many centuries ago.

Pride and sorrow combine in the cenotaph built by one father for his son who died at the age of 20 in the Corinthian War, depicted in bronze, on horseback, triumphing over the enemy. Bonds of family inspired many of the scenes found in the cemetery: The grave terrace of two sisters, and a sculpture of a husband and wife taking tender farewll of each other. One stele found here displayed the carving of a boxer's head, complete with cauliflower ear and leather gloves. There are intensely human scenes of the dead with their pets: A little girl with her dog, a boy with a bird, individual statues of other creatures.

Perhaps the most touching discovery made at this cemetery, however, was the sculpture of a woman and boy with this inscription: "I hold the loved child of my daughter, who used to sit on my knees when we lived in the light; dead now, I hold his corpse."

A grandmother's grief for a dead child melts barriers of time and space. In Kerameikos Cemetery on a quiet Sunday afternoon we felt past and present merge in a common humanity.

Delphi was the center of the world. Here was the sacred stone "omphalos", the navel, the center of the earth. (From the Chinese to the Cherokees, haven't most people defined their land as the center and themselves as the "chosen ones," the "real people" of the earth?)

We may not agree with ancient Greeks about the location of the world's navel, but we cannot dispute that nature and humans have conspired to make Delphi one of the earth's dramatic sites. Arriving there on two different occasions, I felt each time that I had come to a place where human aspiration equalled the magnificence of the natural setting.

Approach up the rugged mass of Mt. Parnassus is slow and scenic. It rises like a bleak, rock fortress broken only by occasional small olive groves on the lower slopes and on the upper heights by clumps of clutching evergreens. The village of Delphi clings to the mountainside, its steep walkways between the upper and lower streets bordered with colorful geraniums and pyracantha and grape arbors. Along the narrow streets huge tourist buses rumble like awkward dinosaurs treading through a rabbit warren. When two dinosaurs meet one must retreat, and which shall yield the passage sometimes is a matter for macho dispute.

But all such problems fade into insignificance in the presence of ancient Delphi, where awesome precipices provide a theater for confronting the mysterious and sacred nature of existence. Poised on this mountainside between the sky which may be dark with lowering clouds or arching in a high, blue radiance, and the distant lowland plain of human planting and harvesting, Delphi seems throughout its history to have inspired worshippers. Mother Earth and Poseidon, god of the sea, were at its legendary birth. From the first there was also an oracle to advise fumbling humans in their choices and decisions. Through the centuries impressive temples were built and treasuries (which held the religious offerings of various cities), altars, a theater, a stadium. Impressive as the remaining rotunda, columns, pediments, foundations, and restored Athenian Treasury may be, capturing our awe and imagination, they nevertheless appear small, even frail, against the mighty backdrop of the mountain.

It was the famous oracle of Delphi who brought pilgrims from as far away as Asia and Egypt and from every corner of Greece to learn the will of the gods. Having sacrificed an animal they awaited the message of the priestess who purified herself in the Castalian Spring, chewed a laurel leaf, and placed herself in the innermost shrine of the Temple of Apollo, near the "omphalos" stone. Her mutterings, not unlike those of many sage political and cultural advisers today, were usually incoherent and always required interpretation which, in turn, often obscured rather than clarified the meaning.

Three vivid memories of Delphi remain with me. One is the story of the rich king, Croesus, who asked the oracle if he would win a war against Persia. Told that he would

258

destroy a mighty empire, he proceeded to wage war — only to discover that the destroyed empire was his own.

The second memory combines the grace and strength of the statue of the bright-eyed Charioteer in the Delphi Museum with the admonitions Plato saw in the shrine at Delphi: Know Thyself. Nothing In Excess.

The third memory is of the senses. Early one morning in Delphi I walked out among the ruins and restorations and saw thin columns of smoke drifting up toward the mountain tops. A pungent aroma rode on the brisk morning air. I half expected to see a priestess fresh from the cold Castalian waters divining some ancient message. Instead, I came upon a group of black-clad women tidying up terraces and walkways, burning brush. Unlike other Greeks I had encountered they did not respond to smiles or nods, made no move to communicate with the stranger, and after brief glances returned to their brush and fires. Sight and smell of the smoke, the dark stern faces of the keepers of this site, put me in elemental touch with Delphi. Stone and smoke: lofty spiritual interludes wedded to patient daily labors.

The Greek islands. Each one boldly different from the others. Rhodes with its arrogant ramparts, echoes of Crusades, knightly armor, and conquest. Santorini, also known as Thera, set like a sparkling jewel in the sea, bonded by earthquake and volcano to magnificent Minoan Crete with its powerful art of bulls, graceful dolphins, acrobats, and its present fruitful groves. Strange, uninhabited Delos and its avenue of great stone lions poised in a roaring that remains forever mute. And Mykonos, all white and black, light and shadow, hills and windmills and chapels, winding passage-ways that were built for confusion and secrecy.

These and many others, large and small, each as jealous of its uniqueness as each Greek person is jealous of his/her individuality.

The departing plane circled above the shimmering sea and the random clusters of islands. Beauty and wisdom: treasures I had expected to find in Greece. I was not disappointed. I recalled a message received over the centuries from a citizen of Rhodes: "I will reveal to you a love potion, without medicine, without herbs, without any witch's magic; if you want to be loved, then love."

And the words of Menander: "He only lives, who living enjoys life."

The morning was chilly. Frost had etched the brown stalks and dying grasses of garden and pasture with sharp clear lines. It had drawn a white film over some of the leaves of the big old oaks and the rooftops of houses. An early breeze that blew along the hillside and stirred the green heavy limbs of the tall pine trees was tinged with a hint of winter's ice to come.

But the sky was blue and clear above the mountains. Sunlight reflected off the tall straight trunks of poplars and the polished surface of dark rhododendron leaves and the swift water of the stream.

I was prowling along the edges of the stream, finding momentary amnesty from pressures of schedule and conscience. Flowing water is restful and refreshing in a very special way. I have turned to it often when I needed a nourishment not to be found in any human concoctions or devices.

How good it was to look down the course of the stream, watch its winding beneath grey boulders and under gnarled roots exposed beneath the overhanging banks of earth. Everywhere were signatures of the patience and persistence of water wearing away dirt banks, tumbling rocks, changing course.

At one sharp turn in the stream I found a wedged stone blocking the flow of water. Sticks, twigs, leaves caught there had created an impromptu dam which was forcing the water to cut farther and farther into the banks. Soon the ferns and small plants there would be washed away. I climbed down to the streambed to move the stone. It was even larger than its upthrust edge had indicated. I could not dislodge it easily. I needed some leverage.

I cleared away sticks and leaves. A jagged edge of the stone became visible. It provided a handle. After a few tugs the stone was loosened and tumbled to the side of the stream. The water washed deep and free through its natural channel.

I thought about the blocks that hinder people in their growth and freedom. We need new leverage. Are there levers we are overlooking which could roll aside some of the trivia, the debris, the barriers, which block us from the mainstream of experience and fullest participation in that mainstream? Winter is a good season for rediscovering mountain brooks.

A century ago an observer who had lived among several Indian tribes stated the attitude and spirit reflected in Chero-

261

kee myth. This man wrote, "I have often reflected on the curious connexation which appears to subsist in the mind of an Indian between man and the brute creation . . . Although they consider themselves superior to all other animals and are very proud of that superiority; although they believe that the beasts of the forest, the birds of the air, and the fishes of the waters were created by the Almighty Being for the use of man," the writer found that the Indians did not set an unbridgeable gulf of difference between humans and all other life. "All animated nature, in whatever degree, is in their eyes a great whole from which they have not yet ventured to separate themselves."

Seasons of the past decade have brought me to closer appreciation of that "great whole" from which I would not separate myself.

Have you ever written — or even read — a letter to a tree? This is a letter to the elm tree that stands at the corner of my house.

Old Friend:

After the big wet snow that surprised our town and county recently I walked outside to become part of a strange new world in which every familiar thing was transformed with beauty and the smallest leaf and twig was highlighted with a coating of unblemished white. As I explored I discovered that one of your large limbs, my favorite one, was cracked under the weight of the snow.

The limb, which always appeared to me as a giant arm bending toward the ground in a graceful embrace before it thrusts upward, had not broken. Old and brittle, suffering under an unexpected burden, it had splintered like bone beneath the skin of its bark still holding bone and sinew together. But it had not fallen. Old friend, I salute you.

And I remember.

I remember springtime when you have never failed to push early green tendrils toward the sun, reaffirming the rebirth of a glorious fresh foliage from the bare winter hibernation.

I remember awakening in early morning light to the busy life taking place within your leafy protection. Robins building a nest one year kept the air lanes busy with their thrifty nest-building and hatching and feeding. And when the young robins made their first flights from your limbs they sometimes tumbled to the ground before discovering their awkward balance and strength of wings. A flicker called your limbs home for several years and I rejoiced in the flash of grey and white and black accented by precisely the right crest of crimson as this haughty tenant became a neighbor.

How many summer afternoons I have returned to your presence, seen your graceful branches rising upward like a green fountain and found refreshment for the spirit. How many crystal-cold nights I have looked through the India ink etching of your twigs toward a moon riding high in the winter sky.

One Easter a sister-in-law sat on the gray stone slab someone long ago placed at your trunk and we watched as our small children discovered colored eggs we had hidden behind every shrub and tree and hedge. She died untimely young but the memory of her happy smile that day is still clear in my mind.

One autumn day the poet in our family sat on that stone with a sheaf of papers and someone snapped his picture. In woolly sweater and comfortable woods-shoes, with the benedication of your lowest limb sweeping close to his head bowed over the pages you and he are captured forever in a special harmony.

Old friend, your roots run deep into the earth and into my life.

May the crack that has come with age and a heavy burden mend and permit the spring sap to flow through your arteries again. But if that limb should break and fall, as you will someday, you have shared to the fullest in life, sheltering, nurturing, inspiring creatures great and small. A blessing you have been. Blessings to you.

Some of my explorations have led down dark paths. But there is still laughter and work and the question, Why? George Bernard Shaw spoke for me when he wrote:

"This is the true joy in life, the being used for a purpose recognized by yourself as a mighty one; the being thoroughly worn out before you are thrown on the scrap heap; the being a force of Nature instead of a feverish selfish little clod of ailments and grievances complaining that the world will not devote itself to making you happy."

He left me a very special legacy, one that only he could have created. He explored a simple incident and made it into a metaphor for death and killing, life and love. I share his gift with you.

The Mate
by
James Stokely

I was only sixteen
And sat trying not to cry in the woods.
I had had no luck
And the October sun was nearly gone.
Uncle Rance, over to my right,
Already had a dozen partridges,
And Lute McSween, a quarter of a mile to the left,
A brace of ducks.
I stood up, wiped my eyes,
And tiptoed into a little clearing
With only the sound of hidden insects
To accompany my ritual stalk and breath.
Suddenly my heart leaped into my hand
As I saw a movement not fifty feet away
The sunlight filtering through the leaves
To envelop the gorgeous creature
In a golden-brown haze,
Strange, proud scion of sky and earth,
Its neck firm and erect,
Its tuft of wing flecked with a lost-world tint
Of rainbow trout in a pool of ferns.
There was no sound
But the beating of two wild hearts.
With the ancient thirst ripe within me
My finger squeezed the lock of my 20-gauge
And the long-tailed ring-necked pheasant
Surprised in its solitary foraging
Collapsed like a rag doll.
The prize was mine!
Why did I not move?
I saw something greenish-blue and red
Come running from the brush
In a frenzy of clucking
Speaking to the lump of bone, flesh, and feathers,
Seeking to lead it to safety.
Rance called from the farther hill
But I did not answer.
I looked at my gun.
The woods and the bird and I
Were equally still.

WITHDRAWN